# GREED

## INVESTMENT FRAUD
## IN CANADA AND
## AROUND THE GLOBE

DEBORAH THOMPSON

VIKING

VIKING
Published by the Penguin Group
Penguin Books Canada Ltd, 10 Alcorn Avenue, Toronto, Ontario,
Canada M4V 3B2
Penguin Books Ltd, 27 Wrights Lane, London W8 5TZ, England
Viking Penguin, a division of Penguin Books USA Inc., 375 Hudson Street,
New York, New York 10014, U.S.A.
Penguin Books Australia Ltd, Ringwood, Victoria, Australia
Penguin Books (NZ) Ltd, cnr Rosedale and Airborne Roads, Albany,
Auckland 1310, New Zealand

Penguin Books Ltd, Registered Offices: Harmondsworth,
Middlesex, England

First published 1997
1 3 5 7 9 10 8 6 4 2

Printed and bound in Canada on acid free paper ⊗

**Canadian Cataloguing in Publication Data**

Thompson, Deborah, 1957–
Greed: investment fraud in Canada and around the globe

ISBN 0-670-87028-5

1. Fraud. 2. Corporations—Corrupt practices. 3. Commercial crimes. I. Title

HV6691.T48 1997      364.1'63      C96-931456-6

Visit Penguin Canada's web site at **www.penguin.ca**

To the Crown counsel, securities regulators
and police investigators across Canada, and to their
counterparts in the United States and around the
globe, who fight investment fraud every day.

# ACKNOWLEDGEMENTS

If someone had told me that one day I would write a book about investment fraud sparked by the fact that I knew someone personally who had committed the crime, I wouldn't have believed them. But I've learned that truth is stranger than fiction. This book is also proof that I have been very fortunate to have had many people help me in this endeavour, and I wish to thank them.

Norman Inkster, president of KPMG Security and Investigation Inc., allowed me countless hours to interview several of his talented staff, in particular: James Hunter, Don Svendson, Michael Deck, Chris Mathers, Helen Ehlers, James McAuley, Derek Rostant and Ross Oake.

Gary Moulton and Stuart Douglas of Deloitte & Touche,

# GREED

David Selley and Don Holmes of Ernst & Young and Neil St. John of Coopers & Lybrand also gave of their valuable time. Diana Chant, a partner at Price Waterhouse, was very helpful, too, and I thank her.

Glenn Higginbotham and Ron Belanger of the Bank of Montreal were most accommodating with their time and expertise, and private investigator Tony Slot gave me helpful insights into the world of scam artists and boiler rooms. U.S. Postal Inspector Michael Hartman and Assistant U.S. Attorney Gordon Zubrod, both of Pennsylvania, also had much to reveal on the subject.

The Reverend Canon Timothy Elliott and the Reverend Dr. Frank Brisbin—both of whom I count among my friends—offered thoughtful comments on issues of ethics and society. Elizabeth Loweth of the Canadian Centre for Ethics & Corporate Policy was an enthusiastic participant on the subjects, as well. The time I spent with Sir Graham Day was fascinating, and his views on corporate governance were thought-provoking and, at times, very amusing. I look forward to meeting with him again some day.

I am deeply indebted to Jay Naster, Crown counsel with the Ontario Ministry of the Attorney General, who was wonderful to work with and very generous with his time. I must also thank defence lawyer David Humphrey of Greenspan, Humphrey in Toronto, who sits on the other side of the fence from Jay, as it were, but was equally accessible and helpful. In addition, lawyers Ray Flett and Gary Clewley provided comments which were most revealing and constructive. Fred Siemens and Bob Purves, both formerly of the Winnipeg Commodity Exchange, were also extremely interesting to interview. Their devotion to

# Acknowledgements

the integrity of the markets was clear and their views highly informative. Economist Patricia Mohr of Scotiabank took time from her hectic schedule to help me with questions I had about commodities.

I have the utmost respect and admiration for the many police officers I contacted for the book. I would especially like to thank: Inspector Walter Somers, Cpl. Brian Carlson, Inspector Earl Moulton, Sgt. John Sliter, Cpl. Rick Edwards and Sgt. Brian Tario—all of whom are with the Royal Canadian Mounted Police. The Ontario Provincial Police were just as accommodating, and I wish to thank Inspector Harold Rose, and Sgts. Jim Wilson and Ed Krajcir. Inspector Stephen Harris of the Metropolitan Toronto Fraud Squad was also very informative.

Dr. Peter Collins of Toronto's Clarke Institute of Psychiatry, Dr. Paul Babiak of New York and Tibor Barsony of the Canadian Foundation of Compulsive Gambling offered compelling insights into the psychological aspects of fraud.

Boston-based analyst Jeoffrey Hall of Technical Data not only provided me with information on the markets, he practically swam to the courthouse during one of Boston's worst floods to pick up important transcripts for me. Thank you, also, to his assistant, Matthew. Court reporter James Gibbons and business staff at *The Boston Globe* were very helpful and quick to provide me with key information for my research.

Securities regulators and authorities across Canada and the U.S. were extremely forthcoming and provided assistance whenever I needed it. In particular, I would like to thank: Larry Waite, Mark Gordon and Brian Butler of the Ontario Securities Commission Enforcement Branch. Dean Holley and Mark Skwarok, formerly of the British Columbia Securities Commission, also provided me with valuable information and made me feel most welcome when I visited them in Vancouver. The Commission's Martin Eady was a tremendous help, too. John Carson, Fredric Maefs, Ralph Shay and Steve Kee of the Toronto Stock Exchange were just as accommodating. Joe Oliver of the Investment Dealers Association of Canada not only met with me to offer his views, he also came up with some interesting ideas for the book. Thank you, too, to staff at the U.S. Securities and Exchange Commission.

Douglas Goold, columnist at *The Globe and Mail*, willingly lent me his only copy of the *Report of the Board of Banking Supervision Inquiry into the Circumstances of the Collapse of Barings* in exchange for a mere lunch. Photographer Peter Redman of *The Financial Post* was also very accommodating (I gave him a box of doughnuts). The years former colleague Stephen Burns of *Bridge News* (previously *Knight-Ridder Financial News*) spent in Tokyo also came in handy. He shed light on the Daiwa and Sumitomo stories for me—all for a couple of beers and a steak (seems to be a feeding pattern here with my journalist friends).

I would also like to thank Steve Newman for his help in the very early stages of the project, as well as Steve Stober for his keen photographic eye.

I have been particularly fortunate to have met and worked with two exceptionally talented editors, Meg Masters at Penguin Canada, and Mary Adachi, who not only fed me while she showed me ways to improve my work, but also provided the moral support of her four "kitty kids." Louise Curtis was another wonderful help to me. Thank you all.

On a personal note, I would like to express my gratitude to

# Acknowledgements

my parents, the late Libbie Brady and my dad, Charlie Brady. When I was growing up, my mother would tell me when I hit what I thought was an insurmountable wall that "Every knock is a boost." I now know what she meant, and she was right. She also showed me the magic of words and reading. My father taught me and my siblings how to enjoy talking to people— from princes to paupers—and I feel his lesson enriched all of our lives. I also believe the verbal bun-throwing that went on around our dinner table with my brothers and sisters, Bill, Kathleen, Carole, Pat and Lorne, sharpened my communication skills.

I have been blessed with very supportive friends, and I would especially like to thank: Margaret Bream, Christine and Michael Carlson, Arlene FitzPatrick, Peter Howell, Gail Lickfold, Kitty Macaulay, Helen McGill, Beatrice Pereira, Sharon Sampson, Malcolm Sinclair and John Sweeney. There are two special friends to whom I owe a very deep debt of gratitude: John Coles and Tim Reid. Thank you for your friendship.

I could not have attempted this book without the hard work and dedication of my children's nanny, Cynthia Aguilar. She saw to it that I had plenty of privacy and quiet time, and only once did my four-year-old son, Samuel, beat us to my ringing office phone. (He had an interesting conversation with an officer from the RCMP.) My daughter, Elizabeth, an avid reader, was particularly keen that I worked "for the penguin book company." I am very proud of my children, and their patience and love are an inspiration to me.

Finally, I cannot say enough about the love and consideration my husband, Bob McWhirter, showed me throughout the entire project. As an investment manager his insights were invaluable to me, and his technical expertise a tremendous help. This has not been an easy task for many reasons, but my husband's unwavering support allowed me to achieve a challenging goal. I will always remember what he did for me, and cherish what we share in our life together.

Deborah Thompson
Toronto, Ontario
January 1997

# CONTENTS

# INTRODUCTION

James Lake was a valued and highly regarded employee of the Toronto-based real-estate firm of J.J. Barnicke Ltd. The thirty-five-year-old was seen as a rising star by his colleagues, family and friends. He enjoyed a close, almost son-like relationship with his boss, realtor Joseph Barnicke, and as chief financial officer, Lake was in charge of payroll and had control over all employee tax slips, including his own. He was considered to be the company's financial watchdog—it was a trusted position.

Lake earned a good, but not spectacular, salary of $100,000 per year, made up of a base of $90,000 and an annual bonus of $10,000. To many who knew him, his income from work was almost inconsequential when set against the money they believed he lived on and enjoyed through a family inheritance.

He, his wife, Elizabeth, and their three young children, in fact, appeared to live a charmed life. The family spent their weekends and leisure time throughout the year at a spectacular 14,000-square-foot home on a beautiful tree-lined property on Balsam Lake, about a two-hour drive northeast of Toronto. Their main residence, just north of Toronto, was equally impressive and furnished with the best money could buy. According to a family acquaintance, "The homes are stunning, just beautiful. It was obvious that they had and chose nothing but the best. Everything was perfection."

But everything was not perfection. The façade of wealth hid a reality that James Lake couldn't ultimately bear to reveal. Until mid-March 1996, things had been going very well for him, but around this time Joe Barnicke received a phone call from a money manager at a large and respected investment management firm in Toronto, who was hired to look after the Barnicke family personal accounts. He asked him why there had been requests on February 6, February 20 and March 14 to move a total of $1.5 million to the company's operating accounts. Barnicke had no idea what the transfers were about, so he went to see Lake, since he was the keeper of the company's finances. Lake told his boss he'd look into the matter and get back to him as soon as possible. Early the next week Barnicke pressed Lake for an answer. Lake told Barnicke that he needed to go to his office to retrieve some documentation to explain the situation, and excused himself. Moments later, however, James Lake fled his downtown Bay Street office, leaving behind his jacket and identification. Late that night Lake's wife notified the police that her husband was missing—he hadn't come home and no one at his office knew where he had gone. The following day she identified her husband's body at the city morgue. James Lake had committed suicide by leaping from a subway platform into the path of an oncoming train.

A subsequent investigation found that Lake had siphoned off more than $2 million a year from the company and had hidden his fraudulent transactions by paying taxes on the money that he sidelined to himself. The temptation to steal overpowered James Lake but, in the end, it was shame that did him in.

"Ex-trader linked to copper scandal arrested in Tokyo"
*The Globe and Mail*
"Ex-RBC Dominion broker pleads guilty to fraud, theft"
*The Financial Post*
"Leeson's bid to be a star led to Barings crash"
*The Financial Times* (London)
"Anatomy of a fraud — How Kurzweil's straight-arrow CEO went awry"
*Business Week*

It seems almost everywhere you look these days someone is being nabbed for lying and cheating their way into corporate funds or somebody's pockets. Hardly a week goes by without a headline pointing to a story about a once-devoted worker, top executive, investment professional, community leader or common criminal accused of committing fraud. Authorities say the crime is pervasive, and in some ways it's getting worse.

The Royal Canadian Mounted Police estimate that cross-border telemarketing scams between provinces and between

# GREED

Canada and the U.S., for example, swindle hundreds of millions of dollars from investors annually. Robert Pitofsky, chairman of the U.S. Federal Trade Commission, says Canada's more lenient consumer protection laws have attracted scam artists who prefer to set up shop "in a nice place like Ontario," and other provinces, rather than in the U.S.

There are equally troubling inter-provincial problems, too. It is estimated that in 1995, for example, Alberta residents lost about $10 million to telephone fraudsters operating out of Quebec. The problem is that Quebec police won't pursue con artists unless their victims reside in the province of Quebec. Other forms of fraud on the rise include the use of bogus credit cards and theft of credit identity, as well as fraudulent-stock promotion on the Internet.

These sorts of frauds present massive legal and regulatory headaches to the authorities. As global market borders blur, it has become increasingly difficult to define jurisdictions, let alone police them. "The role of self-regulation is going to become even more important in the future for several reasons," says Joe Oliver, president of the Investment Dealers Association of Canada. "First, there are fiscal constraints, which means that governments are just not allocating enough funds. Adequate surveillance and investigation of problems relating to the securities business, such as compliance and enforcement, has to, in part, be done by self-regulatory bodies.... The general complexity of the marketplace and the need for more expertise and higher standards is another reason. We are doing our job, but the job is getting bigger."

In some respects experts say the world is becoming the scam artist's oyster. "It's almost like the invisible hand of the markets and the invisible hand of fraud will find where the money is.

# Introduction

That's where the fraudsters go," says James Hunter, a partner and forensic accountant at KPMG Investigation and Security Inc. in Toronto. "If you wanted to do a lightning-rod test for where major frauds are carried out, look to the major capital centres in the world. If you did a survey of where the major frauds have been perpetrated in the last ten years, you've got Singapore, with Nick Leeson and Barings, the Daiwa [Bank] out of New York, Sumitomo out of Tokyo, and the big Canadian ones tend to be in Toronto."

If the Barings Bank and James Lake cases are examples of the extreme, there are thousands of less dramatic, run-of-the-mill frauds that go on every day. According to research done by KPMG, the typical white-collar criminal is usually a man twenty-six to forty years old who earns $50,000 or less. Women commit fraud, too, but are not nearly as likely as men to do so, partly because frauds tend to be committed by people in authority. Simply put, there are fewer females in high-level jobs. The average take by non-management employees is around $26,000, which is not exactly chicken feed, while managers who commit fraud swindle about $40,000 on average from the company. "This discovery seems unexpected, given the recent media coverage of high-profile, large-dollar frauds committed by senior managment," says Norman Inkster, former commissioner of the RCMP and now president of KPMG Investigation and Security Inc. KPMG found that only about 4 per cent of frauds are committed by employees with an annual salary of $100,000 or more, and those over fifty-five rarely take money from company or customer coffers. That's why someone like Christopher Horne, a former RBC Dominion Securities broker who earned well over six figures annually and is in his fifties, is an extremely rare breed. He was convicted of defrauding more than $7 million of client funds.

Although some cases are complex, fraud experts say that most scams are fundamentally simple, nowhere near the mastermind plans deftly executed in television and movie dramas. Gary Moulton, a veteran forensic accountant and partner at accounting firm Deloitte & Touche in Toronto, says, "Ninety per cent [of fraud] is not innovative. It's just bad controls. The controls are there, but they're not being adhered to."

KPMG's Inkster agrees and says that most frauds are not the "headline-grabbing kind" like Horne's, "but, clearly, fraud is a problem that affects a significant number of companies." KPMG estimates that top-tier Canadian companies alone lose more than $1 billion annually to fraud, and that doesn't include the hundreds of millions of dollars individuals forfeit to bogus investment schemes or credit-card theft. A recent survey conducted by the company found that just over half of Canada's 1,000 largest companies reported that fraud had taken place in their organizations in the previous year.

Their international survey, which included 19,000 corporations from eighteen countries across several industries, found that only a small majority of KPMG's Canadian, U.S. and European clients felt that fraud was on the rise. However, a significant majority of their clients in both Africa and Hong Kong believed that fraud was getting worse. Ironically, most clients in the United Kingdom, home of the Barings, Flemings and Robert Maxwell scandals, to name only a few, believed that fraud was on the decline. A number of British respondents said that companies were becoming more aware of and therefore more vigilant about curbing wayward employees. The majority of respondents from the Australasian region believed that fraud was levelling off and would stay about the same in the near future.

Almost one in five of the survey's participants said that they were unwilling to do business in countries and regions that included: Africa, Asia, Brazil, the Caribbean, China, Eastern Europe, India, Iran, Mexico, the Middle East, Russia and, notably, the U.S. Nigeria continues to be the country in which the highest number of respondents refuse to do business.

Survey results also showed that *all* of the South African and German clients with global operations had been victims of fraud. In total, about one-quarter of the companies surveyed indicated that they had faced some form of international fraud that included kickbacks or secret commissions, cheque, credit-card and money-transfer fraud.

The difficulty with all of these findings and large dollar figures, however, is that it's hard for the average person to relate to them—why should anyone care about these numbers?

The answer is that, contrary to what many people think, business fraud—*the* white-collar crime—is not victimless. It could happen to anyone or to almost any company. Individually, entire life savings can vanish, and those taken in by fraudsters are often left both financially and emotionally devastated. In fact, victims who lose money by investing in bogus schemes are usually made to feel as though they deserved it because, they are told, they were greedy. But that's not the primary reason why most people get hooked—it's usually because they're too trusting. As one unfortunate woman, who invested and lost close to $50,000 through a penny-stock scheme, says, "If I am guilty of anything it's that I was naïve and gullible, not greedy." Fraud also weakens institutions and erodes corporate profits, which ultimately pressures economies.

At its very core, fraud involves some of our most basic human characteristics: fear, ego and greed. Astute fraudsters play on victims' fears. "If you don't buy now, you'll miss out on the opportunity of a lifetime," they claim. "Don't tell your wife you lost your nest egg, just buy this stock and you'll make your money back without her knowing," a harassed investor is told. Fraudsters fear being caught, but as time passes and they're not found out, their fear tends to dissipate and, in fact, they can become rather cocky.

Ego plays a dominant role with both the fraudster and the victim. Each successful act of fraud feeds the criminal's ego, which motivates them to commit more fraud, which feeds back into their ego. It's a cycle that ends only when the fraudster is caught or, in rare cases, when they choose to stop. Conversely, the potential for ego-bruising embarrassment usually prevents victims from talking about how they were bilked out of their investments. Most are also too ashamed to even tell family and friends that they've been cheated. However, there is some consolation; even sophisticated and savvy investors can be deceived.

A case that illustrates this point happened in the spring of 1996. It involved a prosperous and well-liked New York real-estate lawyer, David Schick, who was accused of misappropriating millions of dollars from real-estate investors and institutional backers. In fact, out of several civil lawsuits filed against Schick, one was issued by a group of investors which included Albert Friedberg, a highly regarded guru of world currency and commodity markets.

The scandal sent shock waves through Manhattan's Orthodox Jewish community of whom Schick was a prominent member.

# Introduction

He had built much of his fortune through his business contacts and friendships there. Schick even played host at a fundraiser that U.S. President Bill Clinton attended. Because it was an election year, Clinton's aides felt it prudent to release a statement saying the president hadn't engaged in any business deals with Schick. Similarly, most of the victims in this case kept quiet about their financial misadventure rather than risk embarrassment and criticism.

But this is typical in fraud. People who've unwittingly associated with fraudsters through business or social channels can be very harshly treated by others—even when there is clearly no complicity. That's a key reason why the majority of victims don't talk about it. Society judges us by the company we keep—so much so that people have been ridiculed, even ostracized, because of their perceived inability to detect that their colleague, friend or spouse was committing a fraud.

In addition to the money they steal, fraudsters also enjoy basking in the power they hold over people and relish passing themselves off as kind, capable and diligent people. In a corporate setting, they're the employees who regularly work late, or start their days unusually early. They prefer not to take vacations, and will even boast about it. The reality is that the fraudsters can't afford to stay away from their scams too long—they are their lifeblood. Ironically, their "devotion" to work can make distinguishing the fraudster from the honest employee a real challenge for management.

As much as fear and ego play a part in fraud, greed plays the pivotal role. It's the fraudster's prime motivator, says Dr. Peter Collins, a forensic psychiatrist at the Clarke Institute in Toronto. "I have a very simplistic division of what I perceive in human behaviour when it comes to criminality: they're either bad or they're mad. For those who commit heavy-duty fraud, I think the underlying description is that they're greedy. Among those people who commit fraud I've seen some who truly are personality-disordered, some of whom are high-functioning psychopaths, but most are just greedy."

Dr. Collins says it may be a simple answer to what motivates the fraudster, "but it's accurate." The flashy cars, beautiful homes and speedboats become too important to give up, Dr. Collins says, and that's why they pursue their fraudulent activities.

There are other reasons why some turn to the crime. There are those who've racked up huge debts, or need to feed a drug or gambling habit. One expert says some gamblers—at least to the outside world—exhibit similar personality traits to those seen in fraudsters.

Like most fraudsters, "gamblers try to conduct an image of self-confidence to the world. They create a happy-go-lucky façade," explains Tibor Barsony, executive director of the Ontario branch of the Canadian Foundation of Compulsive Gambling. But many gamblers "haven't the ability to deal with reality and they become habitual liars to the level that they themselves believe their lies. That becomes their reality."

According to Barsony the investment and banking industries are ideal havens—but not the exclusive domain—for people with an inclination to gamble. "Where else but in the investment world can you get paid to make bets?" Barsony asks. Faced with shrinking financial resources, a compulsive gambling habit can push people to commit fraud. Of course, most gamblers don't go as far as former assistant bank manager Brian Malony, who in the early '80s lost more than $10.2 million of his employer's money.

# Introduction

Malony's penchant for gambling was so extreme that he was known to make multiple wagers on the wins and losses of football teams he knew absolutely nothing about. One casino accommodated his habit by regularly flying the Toronto-based banker to and from Las Vegas in a Lear jet. Although through psychological testing he was deemed to be a gambling addict, he was sentenced to six years in prison for his deeds.

In another case, a portfolio manager at a Pennsylvania bank in the early '90s began buying volatile fixed-income futures and then keeping the buy-and-sell orders, known as tickets, in his desk drawer for a few days. If he was offside on the bet, he would register it as a loss on his company's trading account. If the gamble made money, the profits were posted in his personal account. Known as "Tickets in Drawer Syndrome," or TIDS, it continues to be a problem despite dramatically improved electronic monitoring and internal controls many investment companies have implemented. The investment manager's win-win record came to an abrupt halt when company officials discovered his drawer antics and he was sentenced to three years in jail.

Despite the best efforts of corporations, regulatory agencies and police, reining in fraudsters is a very tough job. Inspector Walter Somers, head of the Commercial Crime Section, Milton, Ontario, detachment of the Royal Canadian Mounted Police, explains that part of the reason why there has been a rise in recent years in, for example, fraud against individuals is that "there's a generational issue going on. A lot of the victims are older because these are people who've come up through the '30s, '40s and '50s—eras when everyone was more trusting than people are today. The targets that some of these criminals are going after are predisposed to being trusting.... The crime of the future

# GREED

is staying with the greying of America. If you stay focused as a criminal towards the older generation, especially in the white-collar crime area, your chances are much greater for success simply because of the fact that you're dealing with a generation that isn't quite surfing the Internet. They don't have the sophistication that the younger generation has."

Work done by Dr. David K. Foot, an economist and demographer at the University of Toronto, supports Inspector Somers's observations. Dr. Foot also believes that fraud will become much more prevalent as baby boomers grow older. "After armed hold-ups, the next step up the career ladder for a criminal is into fraud: telemarketing scams, forged credit cards, and bogus investment schemes to dupe naive people, often seniors, out of their life savings," he says in his book, *Boom Bust & Echo*. Dr. Foot says that white-collar crime is usually associated with older criminals because there's "a degree of knowledge and sophistication" needed to commit the crime. "And the older criminal, if he wants to stay in business, needs to find less strenuous work. He is less able than his younger colleague to hold up banks and convenience stores because he's not as strong or as fast as he used to be."

Aging criminals may turn to the less physically taxing way in which to make a dishonest living, but, as Inspector Somers says, the baby-boom generation won't be as trusting as their parents' and grandparents' generation, and probably won't be as easily duped.

However, con artists know many effective ways to pry open people's hearts and wallets, especially if the targeted victim is a senior citizen. Scam artists are aware that for an elderly person with limited access to the outside world, or someone who's simply lonely, or looking to build a nest egg, a friendly and "informative" phone call is a very welcome thing.

Another area very much in the fraudster's favour today is the growing global marketplace. Statistics from the Bank for International Settlement, for example, show daily trading in currencies has more than sextupled to about US $1.23 trillion a day, or one hundred times the volume of world trade from a little more than ten years ago when it hovered around US $200 billion a day. In 1985 barely fifty countries had stock markets with a total capitalization of around US $4.7 trillion. There are now more than two hundred stock markets, including the many small markets within Russia and China, for a total capitalization of more than US $16 trillion. Worldwide investment in international mutual funds has multiplied more than thirty-fold in the past decade to reach hundreds of billions of dollars. There is simply more money out there for con artists to go after, so even if a small fraction of this wealth is tied to fraud, the numbers would be staggering.

Certainly, change in the world's traditional banking system was instrumental in the demise of England's Barings plc. The bank's dramatic undoing has been dissected over boardroom and dinner tables ever since Nick Leeson, the infamous "rogue trader," fled Barings' Singapore office in February 1995. Caught in a web of lies and losses that ultimately reached £827 million sterling, or US $1.4 billion, Leeson helped tear down one of the United Kingdom's great bastions of finance. It was the bank where Her Majesty Queen Elizabeth, no less, held money on deposit. And it was the bank whose roots ran so deep that they reached all the way back to 1762, the year Barings was established as a merchant bank—well before Napoleon Bonaparte met his Waterloo.

"I think what Nick Leeson did obviously meant that he was not the most ethical person," KPMG's Hunter says. "But he most likely wouldn't be able to play the same stunt in a smaller centre. Big frauds are attracted to centres of capital.... To me, it's an aspect of the '90s. For example, in that bank twenty years ago somebody from his social background with his relatively young age would never have been put in that position of trust. But because of the pushing down of empowerment, he was given a massive amount of responsibility and in his case he abused it. But he's not totally to blame. The senior people in London were either not paying attention, or they didn't know what was going on.... To me, it's a real object lesson that fraud doesn't occur in a vacuum."

Diana Chant, a partner at Price Waterhouse in Toronto, whose Singapore-based office, along with the Bank of England, conducted an investigation into Barings, believes the subsequent finger-pointing by Barings' senior management clearly indicated a lack of accountability and communication. "The biggest question with Barings was, who knew or ought to have known? It's like someone stealing something out of a cookie jar and then saying: 'It's not my fault, it's your fault, it's the other person's fault.' It really comes down to, who ought to have known," says Chant, an expert in capital markets.

Of course, the speed with which things happened was still another factor. "The interesting thing about Nick Leeson is that it's true that he engineered the fraud over a couple of years, but he brought down the bank in seventeen days," says KPMG's Hunter. "But losses caused by the seventeen-day period of financial straddles caused the bank to collapse." During January and

# Introduction

February 1995, Leeson placed massive long positions in Nikkei 225 Index futures, anticipating a rise in price, and built a large short position in Japanese Government Bond futures, in the belief they would drop in value. What Leeson hadn't counted on was the Kobe earthquake in January 1995, which not only levelled buildings and killed scores of people, but moved the market against all of Leeson's positions. On February 27, like the rubbled edifices of Kobe, the bank collapsed under the weight of his losses. Leeson was ultimately sentenced to six and a half years in a Singapore prison, and is expected to be a free man by the turn of the century.

If people wonder why so many of these shocking frauds keep cropping up, Michael Deck, former associate director of the Centre for Corporate Social Performance and Ethics at the University of Toronto, and now a principal at KPMG, has an explanation. He says that following the corpulent '80s, the '90s heralded a return to a Slim Fast version of company management. Shareholders began demanding better returns and so firms responded by getting rid of jobs, the lion's share of which came from middle management. To make matters worse, those who kept their positions were under even greater pressure to perform. That made some employees realize that as fewer people were minding the corporate store, there was more opportunity—a key ingredient of fraud, experts say—to take home extra bacon courtesy of the company.

"I think one of the things we've seen changing in business is that, for example, twenty years ago there were a lot more people in organizations, there were more layers, and there were, perhaps not consciously applied, more imposed controls. There were managers, and sub-managers and middle managers—what they used to call the span of control. The number of people you had in the immediate next level down from you might have been twenty, whereas with the flattening of organizations that might now be one hundred. You can't watch a hundred people, so one of the things that's happening with organizations flattening out is the ability of the imposed control is greatly diminished. There's more opportunity for people to act fraudulently and unethically," says Deck.

Elizabeth Loweth, executive director of the Canadian Centre for Ethics & Corporate Policy, a nation-wide think-tank on ethics, believes that "downsizing in the '90s" has created "an almost unbearable" situation for workers, which makes her wonder where society is headed.

"If we continue with what *The Economist* calls 'corporate anorexia,' I think what we're going to do is shoot ourselves in the foot. My own theory is that the more you downsize in this sort of hysterical structuring, the more you undermine the underpinnings of society," which allows for more moral decay and the potential for more fraud, Loweth says. *The Economist*'s "point was that we're going to lose creativity and the bottom line is growth in a capitalistic society. I think that if you take that interpretation of growth you are going to find that you do not have creative, new people coming in. You're going to find you're dying on the vine. If we continue on this route, we'll be into a real cycle of downward spiralling," she warns.

Another part of the equation is the growing chasm between what the ordinary rank and file are paid and what corporate bosses are paid, and this has siphoned off some of the corporate loyalty that was far more prevalent among the working masses even a decade ago. As *Globe and Mail* columnist Jeffrey

# Introduction

Simpson noted in the spring of 1996, large executive salaries can be justified when company executives make sound decisions, but there is no justification for inflated paycheques when the firm's stock sinks for a prolonged period of time, or decisions are made which drag profits down. "Somehow the anxious times don't seem to have percolated upward, because the spread between the best-paid and lower-paid employees keeps widening. And few seem to care," he wrote. There is no doubt that when pay gaps widen, many lower-level employees begin to feel resentment towards management, and that can result in some taking matters, office supplies and company money into their own hands.

Frederick Reichheld, author of *The Loyalty Effect: The Hidden Force Behind Growth, Profits and Lasting Value*, suggests that if a company respects and rewards its employees appropriately, the results benefit not only the staff but usually the bottom line, too. Reichheld says that companies with a "loyalty-based management system," which closely tracks key employee-satisfaction factors as incentives, training and career paths, do well because "they treat their employees as assets, rather than costs."

Society's drift away from morality, having moved more swiftly in recent years, is another factor in fraud's rise. "Years ago we knew who did what, and we had a sense of each other's familial roots. We knew if a person came from money, or if they didn't. Likewise in business, corporate origins were widely known, quality was demanded and integrity expected.... But in today's world of borrowed money there are a lot of things that are a house of cards. What looks stable, like [the defunct] Confederation Life and Barings Bank, for example, isn't at all. We've moved into this world where something is not always what it looks like," says the Reverend Canon Timothy Elliott of Christ

Church Deer Park in Toronto. "We've split off the whole sense of community and the common good so it's everybody for themselves and alienation sets in. I'm speaking very generally, but we don't know what the integrity of something is any more. We don't know who owns the company, or who the boss is. The thinking [in theft and fraud] is that nobody's going to notice and it's not going to hurt anybody.... Somebody who's creative with that kind of a bent of mind says nobody really cares because nobody really knows."

Canon Elliott has a point, says KPMG's Hunter, and adds that ethics within an organization starts at the top. "If the tone from the man or woman at the top is not ethical, that is pervasive. It just spreads throughout the organization. That's why in Canada we have banks that have been around for 150 years, because even though the founders may have been narrow-minded and bigoted, they had a pretty clear moral vision. There were certain things that were just not permissible. And their vision—you could say they were all egomaniacs, but maybe they were positive egomaniacs—their vision was pretty clear. If you diverged from the path of righteousness you were toast. And that is what is lacking in a lot of our organizations. The CEOs come and go and people don't really care about ethics. As a result, you're going to get failures of internal control and an atmosphere that allows fraud. It sounds a bit sententious, but I think it's true."

Lynn Paine, an associate professor at the Harvard Business School and a specialist in management ethics, takes an even harder line than Hunter. "Managers who fail to provide proper leadership and to institute systems that facilitate ethical conduct share responsibility with those who conceive, execute and knowingly benefit from corporate misdeeds."

# Introduction

There is no doubt that there are many strong and ethical leaders in corporations around the world, but some would argue they're a dying breed. One who embodies an ideal in moral leadership is Henry Grunfeld, former president of the highly respected, London-based S.G. Warburg, one of the leading investment banks in the world. High finance had been his life for more than six decades, but a year before the grand old gentleman of Threadneedle Street retired in 1995—he was then in his nineties—Grunfeld consented to an interview with *The Financial Times* and offered some insights.

When Grunfeld was head of the firm, his employees saw him as a moral compass, guiding them through the maze of business and ethical challenges that they faced every day. He was a man of honour, and was once even described as having "an oracular stillness" about him. When he left Warburg, his confrères lamented that the likes of him would never be seen again. He had helped build the firm with his friend and lifetime business partner, the late Siegmund Warburg, on a foundation of honesty and fairness.

Grunfeld said he likened his business approach to Victorian political economist Walter Bagehot's concept of constitutional monarchs, "to advise, to encourage and to warn." As Warburg's resident watchdog and mentor he was demanding, but he was also a man capable of showing compassion. "If someone here makes a mistake, we don't sack him, we try to help him so that it doesn't happen again," he told *The Financial Times*.

But Grunfeld also had a pragmatic side in seeking higher levels of business and ethical performance from his employees, although one of his tactics was seen by some in the financial community as bizarre. He was a big believer in using graphology and psychological tests as means to detect personality flaws in prospective employees. He felt that they were effective ways to prevent the company from hiring people inappropriate for the job, or worse, people inclined to steal or commit fraud. In North American corporate circles the tests were viewed as an affront to individual rights to privacy, but like many businessmen of his generation he wasn't particularly concerned about being politically correct.

Grunfeld stumbled onto the use of handwriting tests when he was working in the family steel business in Germany in the 1920s. Some company cash had gone missing and it was thought that one of three, long-term employees had probably stolen it. It was suggested to Grunfeld that he should seek the advice of a handwriting expert. He did, and after having the trio tested, they were able to pinpoint the culprit. The worker confessed, but as Grunfeld said, "We didn't dismiss him and he never did it again."

Without question, to Grunfeld and his contemporaries, the notion of the '90s-created "rogue trader" pulling the trigger on multi-million-dollar deals while running amok with company funds would be unthinkable, if not impossible. Of course, the dilemma we're faced with today is, it's not only possible, it's reality.

In the chapters that follow, a variety of fraud cases—from those that have had a dramatic impact on world markets to others of more local infamy—are explored. Although they are different in many ways, there's one common thread throughout: in their wake each has left tremendous personal and financial devastation. The victims have endured monetary ruin, ill health, broken families and a loss of trust in humanity that few feel will be fully restored. Corporate reputations have been bruised and the cost to pursue the fraudsters has been huge. Literally, millions of dollars have been spent, and in several cases, the authorities are still in the process of bringing the criminals to justice.

# —1—

# ALL THAT GLITTERS

G reed is at the wheel of most investment scams, experts say, but fear is a welcome passenger that rides along with it on the road to ruin. Driven by greed, fraudsters know that to get to their destination—money—they must encourage their victims' sense of fear. At first, victims fear that they will lose out on an opportunity in a seemingly "legitimate investment." But then, another kind of fear takes over—fear of having to tell family and friends that they've been duped. However, telling the people you love that you've been conned and innocently lost your savings is one thing. Telling them, when you're a man of the cloth, that *you*'ve deceived people in order to get money, then invested those funds in something that you believed to be genuine—but wasn't—is entirely another thing.

The chilly morning in early 1993 started out for U.S. Postal Service Inspector Michael Hartman in his Harrisburg,

Pennsylvania, office like any other—phones ringing, people milling about, paperwork piled high. One telephone call was from a lawyer who had some questions he wanted answered on behalf of a client who didn't want to be identified.

The client turned out to be a Lutheran minister who was both a victim and a perpetrator of fraud. The Reverend Robert Finkbeiner "was in a Catch-22. If he notified us of his loss of money, then we'd also find out that he obtained the money by fraud. He was in between a rock and a hard place, so he avoided us [hoping he could avoid U.S. prosecution] and eventually went to the Royal Canadian Mounted Police," says Hartman.

After contacting RCMP officers in the Commercial Crime Section of the force's Newmarket office, north of Toronto, Canadian police were eventually able to persuade Finkbeiner, former president of the Lutheran Social Services in York, Pennsylvania, to tell his shocking story.

The RCMP learned that he had lost US $1.4 million in a gem-stone scam. Unfortunately, it wasn't his money to lose. He had "borrowed" the funds under false pretences from the charity where he worked, as well as from several local banks and a few major contributors to the Lutheran Social Services whom Robert Finkbeiner knew as friends.

Police eventually learned it was a fraud within a massive fraud and that Finkbeiner was only one of 1,900 U.S. citizens swindled out of a total of more than US $30 million. Dragnets set up by U.S. Postal Service and RCMP officers, assisted by local police authorities, ultimately scooped up dozens of accused fraudsters across the U.S. and Canada. The victims not only paid a huge financial price, but many of their families were emotionally and financially torn apart, and the twilight years of some senior citizens who were victims turned into living nightmares.

According to Ron Belanger, who at the time was a sergeant in the Commercial Crime Section of the RCMP, after several telephone conversations with the minister's lawyer and Finkbeiner, "we persuaded him to help identify the group and then we did a search warrant on the premises. We had observed the telemarketers [in a strip mall, in Markham, northeast of Toronto] going to their boiler room and later going to the bank to make large deposits. We finally collected enough evidence to obtain a search warrant." But it was to no avail. The scam suspects had moved out only hours before police arrived. (Belanger is now a theft and fraud investigator with the Bank of Montreal in Toronto.)

"Boiler-room" operations can be traced back as far as the 1930s and 1940s and were so dubbed because they originated in the boiler rooms of run-down, sometimes abandoned, buildings. The cons only needed a few telephone lines, some chairs, a table or two and a list of names to call. Today, boiler-room fraudsters continue to use high-pressure and fraudulent selling tactics on anyone who'll listen, but most have now elevated their locale, at least to the ground-floor level. Boiler-room cons flog just about anything over the phone, but it's almost always worthless goods such as bogus stocks, low-quality gems and valueless strategic metals. Scam artists sell them to what they call "mooches"—or victims.

Canadian fraudsters have the dubious distinction of being masters at the game since telemarketing frauds based in the U.S. were forced to pack up or move north because of previous injunctions, and more recently because of stricter penalties introduced in late 1994 by the Clinton administration. "Boiler rooms are borderless. It's very easy to start one up. You just need

# GREED

a bunch of sleazy salespeople, a row of telephones and a sucker list. The product they're flogging is totally irrelevant, whether it be gemstones or penny stocks," says Mark Gordon, senior legal counsel with the Enforcement Branch of the Ontario Securities Commission. According to the Washington-based National Consumers League, which manages the National Fraud Information Center in the U.S., telemarketing fraud bilks North Americans out of hundreds of millions of dollars every year. Complaints to the centre about Canadian companies' telemarketing practices have risen sharply in recent years, jumping to more than two hundred calls per month in 1996, compared with fewer than twenty per month just two years before.

With the advent of more efficient communications there are even more avenues for crime. The Internet, for example, is now a haven for fraudsters. The cons set up phony Web pages to obtain valuable information from respondents, such as credit-card and bank-account numbers. Authorities discovered one fake Web page that was crafted to appear as if Procter & Gamble was offering consumers product coupons in exchange for personal financial information. In addition, as fraudsters devise more sophisticated business schemes, and focus their cross-border selling on an aging population, boiler-room operations of the '90s have become increasingly difficult for investigators and regulatory authorities to shut down, and too lucrative for fraudsters to give up.

It was in early November 1989 that Robert MacFarlane, also known to police as "John Taylor," incorporated a company in Ontario called Equity Control Exchange Inc. (Marvin Salsky, a partner in the deal, has since died.) A couple of years later MacFarlane created another firm, International Exchange Board

# All That Glitters

Inc. The firms were fronts, numbered companies whose only assets were "sucker" lists. The lists were made up of names of people who had already been duped in a scam about a decade before, and most of whom still weren't aware that they had been conned. Like a chain letter that wouldn't die, the victims' original investments would come back to haunt them.

The investors believed that they had bought legitimate gemstones with real value. In fact, they were poor-quality gems and essentially worthless. The investors saw their purchases as a "long-term" investment—something that would give them wealth, or at least a financial cushion, in their retirement years, and possibly generate enough money to pass on to their children and grandchildren as a legacy.

They were right in a way—it was "long term"—a lifetime of shattered hopes and financial devastation followed. That didn't matter to MacFarlane. Committing fraud provided him with a very comfortable lifestyle without a lot of effort, and he reasoned that if these gullible investors could be duped the first time, they could be duped again. MacFarlane's victims were ripe for a second picking.

Most of the investors were from "small-town America," far away from the hustle-bustle of big urban centres. Many lived in the homes and farms that dot the countryside of mid-state Pennsylvania and surrounding areas such as Adams, Centre, Lycoming, Northumberland and York counties. The majority were from working- to middle-class stock—people who were brought up on strong work ethics and made honest livings. Most weren't interested in or looking for get-rich-quick schemes, nor were they savvy stock- or bond-market investors. The "precious stones" appealed to their sensibilities because they liked the idea

29

that they were investing in something of value that came from the earth. It gave them a sense of comfort—they could look at them and actually feel them.

As with others of his ilk, MacFarlane's primary goal was to bag as much money as he could and then move on. By November 1991 he had his fill and was ready to sell the companies and the sucker lists. Over his years as a con he had come in contact with other scam artists from whom he had bought the valuable name lists. The names of the people, police believe, were originally chosen arbitrarily from telephone books throughout Pennsylvania. "It's incredible, but somebody who was scamming people had the foresight to preserve the original name list," observes Belanger.

When they learned that MacFarlane was hoping to "retire," three of his "employees," Allen Grossman, Eugene Yermus and Michael Schaumer, allegedly agreed to buy the lists from him for a reported US $300,000. Police statistics show that some boiler-room operations can produce returns several times that amount every month. Tony Slot, a recently retired Metropolitan Toronto Fraud Squad police officer who is now a private investigator, says that current police data reveal that "mid-sized boiler rooms alone can gross over US $1 million a month." The men had worked for years as MacFarlane's top "salesmen," also known as "loaders" in the boiler-room industry. ("Loaders" are people who "load up" victims with more bogus goods after they've made an initial purchase.)

Over the next year and a half police say Grossman, Schaumer and Yermus established and operated successor companies: Capital Exchange Board, Associated Overseas Investors Services, Bo-Shek Cutting and Polishing Inc., Fidelity Asset Trading and

# All That Glitters

Gheko Fox Yamoto Capital Management, which appears to be a perverse nod (although spelled differently) to "Gordon Gekko," the character played by Michael Douglas who was the embodiment of greed in the hit movie *Wall Street*. Assistant U.S. Attorney Gordon Zubrod, the lawyer who prosecuted many of those charged in the case, says that he was told that the first three initials of the management company, "GFY," in fact stood for "Go Fuck Yourselves." "It shows the contempt they had for their victims," says Zubrod.

Grossman, also known to police as "Allen Bush," Yermus, known as "Gene Young" and Schaumer, whose alias was "Michael Simon," were apparently equal partners in the companies and victims say they introduced themselves as senior consultants at their various firms. Investors were told that a variety of services could be provided, including a "hard-asset division" made up of coin, stamp-collection, artwork and gemstone investments.

Through the use of telephone call-forwarding and bogus mailing addresses, victims believed that they were dealing with gemstone-investment dealers in Halifax, Nova Scotia, and then, later, dealers in Calgary, Alberta. In reality, the calls were made from offices located in Thornhill and Markham, Ontario. Police say a handful of other telemarketers worked out of Boca Raton, Florida. An indictment filed against the three accused fraudsters by the United States District Court for the Middle District of Pennsylvania charged that the men targeted U.S. citizens "in order to hinder the investigative and prosecutive efforts of law enforcement and regulatory agencies."

"We're not sure exactly how many names they had, but it could have been as many as 4,000. Victims were told [when they originally bought the 'gems'] that if they kept the stones long enough they'd appreciate in value," says Belanger. The "gems" came with a very believable certificate of authenticity and were encased in plastic with a rider that warned the owner not to break the seal, or they would lose the value of the stone.

While the victims' "precious stones" gathered dust in drawers, safety-deposit boxes and under beds over the decade, the accused con artists allegedly prepared to pick up where MacFarlane had left off. Staff began dialling for dollars. "Cert drivers," as Belanger describes them, who are more commonly known as "qualifiers" in boiler-room businesses, were given investor cards with the names of the people who had previously invested in the stones. (Qualifiers simply contact investors to see if they still have their certificates and then ask them to send in more information.) Investors say they were told to mail or fax the details, such as the stone's carat size, number and kind of stones they owned.

The victims were trusting, obedient people, and that's what the qualifiers counted on. Most investors wasted no time in sending the appropriate information. "After they were told that they could probably get a price that was twenty times their original investment—especially when the person might have initially paid US $20,000—they thought they could sell their collection for a few hundred thousand dollars," says Belanger.

The investors, who now believed they would sell their portfolios at a handsome profit, soon became unwitting buyers of more fake stones. They didn't realize—until it was too late—that they'd likely never sell their "gems" for even a fraction of the original price they paid.

In a typical boiler room, qualifiers gather a stack of investor names and information and then hand them over to an "account opener," or a junior salesman. Within a few days the opener calls each investor again and tells the customer that they have another client—usually someone from outside the country—who is "extremely interested" in the collection, but that the prospective buyer would offer a better price if there was "a more complete portfolio of stones." The victim is "always short a ruby or sapphire, or whatever they can get the victim to believe that they need to add," says Belanger. (In fact, a real precious stone is priced by the gem's carat size and quality, according to Birks Jewellers, specialists in gemstones, and the number of stones in a portfolio is immaterial. It's the quality of each gem that counts.)

Victims said they were told that if they didn't buy more stones, their portfolios wouldn't fetch a very good price in the "open market." If they agreed to buy more stones, which the vast majority of them did, they were given the name of a "highly recommended" company, Bo-Shek Cutting and Polishing, which quoted them prices for the gems they wanted to buy. Most investors were not aware that Bo-Shek was a company owned and operated by Grossman, Yermus and Schaumer.

After agreeing to purchase the additional gems, victims said they were told to send a cheque immediately. "In return, I was told that the moment the overseas buyer accepted my portfolio, the funds from the sale would be wired to a neutral account for me," one victim said. In fact, openers were usually so brazen and the scheme so outrageous that many investors were told that their huge profits would be delivered to them by either Brink's, Pinkerton or Wells Fargo Security within thirty days after completion of the sale. Some victims were even convinced that a truckload of money would be dumped on their doorsteps.

But that never happened. In fact, shortly after the victims sent their money to buy more gems, they'd generally be called again by the scam artists. Many were told that the prospective overseas gem buyer had backed out of the deal, and that a search was on for another buyer. Victims said that when they were called with the news that their buyer had dropped out of the deal, they were also told that the original salesman who had contacted them had left the company, or that the salesman had a death in the family. The person calling them claimed to be their "new" sales representative.

Victims said that the "new" salesman, or "loader" used various ploys to gain their sympathy—the gemstone salesman was going through tough times or facing a divorce. The victims were a gullible bunch. The loader would then offer the investor more opportunities to make even "greater profits" while they hunted for another buyer. The victims were told outrageous stories just to keep them on the hook. Sometimes they were offered other "assets," strategic metals such as indium—a metal with very little market value.

If the victim claimed to have no more funds to invest, the loader would "help" by offering his or her "own money" to save the sale. However, several days later the loader would call again to tell the victim that lending personal funds to clients was a violation of securities regulations, or against company rules. The client would be forced to pay more money—funds he or she couldn't afford to lose. The fraudsters were relentless. The cycle of threats and lies continued until the victim realized that he or she had been duped, or the money was all gone.

The webs they spun were so tight that it was impossible for

some investors to escape total financial annihilation. One was a farmer in his eighties who had worked decades to secure a good life for his family. He and his wife, who had been a school teacher, had built a home together in rural Pennsylvania and raised a family of four girls. He made a modest income during most of his working life, but when he sold his farm he finally came into some real money. "Like many of his generation, he invested, but he was always conservative," says one daughter, who requested anonymity for her father and family.

"My father was contacted throughout '87 and '88. It just snowballed from there. They would get him to buy one more gemstone for his portfolio, and then the prices just kept on going higher and higher. I think it was US $23,000 for one gem to complete a package, and then they'd tell him that they would sell his portfolio to overseas investors. When they'd call, they'd say they were working for the Bank of Canada. [The Bank of Canada is not a chartered bank, it's Canada's central bank.] They'd tell him anything to make it sound official. And they would belittle him, and say: 'Why aren't you going to invest $23,000 when you'll make the $435,000 and so many cents when it's done.' The focus of the phone calls was the big amount he was going to make," says his daughter.

"The phone calls would last an hour to an hour and a half at a time. They just droned on. It was like brainwashing. They'd focus on how much he would lose and then tell him that this Brink's truck was going to come and deliver money to the door. He continued investing.... They were very coercive and very belittling. How can you deal with someone who makes fun of you? They'd tell him, 'Why are you so foolish not to take this chance?' Then it became terrible fear, because he realized he had invested all this money and if he didn't invest a little bit more he was going to lose it all," she says. The daughter says her father lived in fear that his money was gone, and then he'd start thinking that he'd have a chance to dig himself out of the mess. At one point the man had several supposedly different companies calling him daily to talk to him about selling his package. "He felt that something important was going on because all these guys wanted his gemstones," says his daughter.

When the man's family finally realized what was happening, they contacted the local Better Business Bureau and were informed that the companies were probably bogus. "My sister contacted the crooks up there and said, 'My father is elderly, you are causing a lot of stress in my family, please stop.' The salesman called my father back and said, 'I'm a V.P. of this company and I do not talk to daughters, I do not talk to wives, I talk to you.' They'd belittle my father something awful. It was unbelievable what my father went through with these crooks."

In the end, her father lost US $150,000, wiping out his *entire* life savings, but the scam took away much more than money. The fraudsters "didn't murder people, but they devastated lives. My father has changed forever. He hasn't any trust in anybody. I don't trust anybody. We, as a family, don't trust our justice system," says his daughter.

But on March 13, 1993, this con came to an end. The RCMP bagged more than one hundred bankers' boxes of evidence including names, addresses and telephone numbers of victims, and the fraudsters' computer system. They eventually discovered that the Markham operation was making, on average, 40,000 phone calls per month to the United States.

RCMP computer technicians were able to extract incriminating information from the confiscated computer's hard drive, which included financial statements and customer lists. The fraudsters "were good enough to do their financial statements accurately and it showed US $22 million had been taken in over the previous twelve months. It gave it to us in a nutshell," Belanger says. Seized documents even provided the aliases of all the people involved in the scam.

Ironically, at this point the RCMP were still unaware that the U.S. Postal Service was also investigating the scam. "With any scheme to defraud, there's a strong potential that the United States mails are used," explains Hartman of the U.S. Postal Service. "There is no straight fraud statute in the federal court system of the United States. It's either mail fraud, wire fraud through interstate telephones or bank fraud. It's hard to avoid the United States mail system in some way, and we started an investigation" after receiving the call from Finkbeiner's lawyer in early 1993.

A few months later, by the summer of 1993, the RCMP's Belanger and Hartman joined forces. They turned out to be a good team. The men had a lot in common, including an interest in hunting and fishing, and most important, a keen desire to "catch the bad guys," says Belanger. A year's worth of phone calls and shared information later, Belanger flew to Harrisburg in July 1994 to meet with Hartman at his office and testify before a grand jury. Although the two men and other investigators on their team had a lot more work ahead of them, another break in the case eventually helped crack it wide open.

After countless hours of painstakingly gathering information, the investigators learned that two salesmen out of the scam operation's Florida office were planning to meet Yermus,

# GREED

Grossman and Schaumer to buy the companies' lists and start yet another "new" operation. Police officers were waiting for the duo when they arrived at Miami airport and arrested them before they were able to board a flight to Canada. At that point "the case really began to fly," says Hartman. "The two U.S. salesmen gave us the leverage we needed because we faced problems with extradition [of the Canadians who were ultimately charged in the case] and the fact that it was a boiler room on Canadian soil. We couldn't just reach out and touch someone. We only had jurisdiction over U.S. citizens [as officers of the U.S. Postal Service]."

"The people at their satellite office in Boca Raton, Florida, decided to cooperate with our investigation," adds Belanger. "A lot of these guys hired attorneys because they were facing long terms in prison, so they gave depositions" in order to plea bargain for reduced sentences.

Many of the accused cons in this case began ratting on others involved in other scams to be granted less jail time. The net result was that a U.S. grand jury ultimately indicted forty-four people, involved in about a dozen bogus companies, for participating in telemarketing scams. Assistant U.S. Attorney Zubrod is credited with doggedly prosecuting the accused, which ended in a significant number of convictions.

"It was decided it would be best if they stood trial in the U.S. because the victims were American," Belanger says. However, a few of the accused, who are Canadian and residing in Canada, continue to avoid extradition to the U.S. and have not yet stood trial. In fact, one of the accused boasted that he had more than enough money to fight extradition proceedings every step of the way.

# All That Glitters

While some cling to Canadian soil, there was one who slipped past police nets entirely. "He's living in Europe. We were one step behind him. He moved all of his assets to Quebec before leaving Canada. The only way they can avoid going to jail is to hide somewhere in the world," says Belanger.

One con who didn't get away, because another fraudster squealed on him, is a Canadian who is currently doing time in the U.S. for a related telemarketing scam. Interviewed from a mini-mum-security prison located in upstate New Jersey, the fraudster asked that his name be withheld to protect his family and possible repercussions from fellow inmates: "Initially, as a salesman [loader] I made between US $1,600 to $2,000 a week. It's very easy to start this kind of business. All you need is a telephone list of names, and you hire a few guys and you can build up an orga-nization in no time. We made US $15,000 to $18,000 a week— did that for fifteen months. You have to eventually move on. At my peak I was making US $25,000 to $30,000 a week, about US $1.5 million a year," he says.

Knowing the system inside and out as he does, the man thinks improvements in the legal system would result in more fraudsters being caught and more boiler rooms being closed. "I wonder if they go after more arrests and convictions because it's better for them or should their motive be to stop crimes before they hap-pen? I think a lot of the police are overworked ... there should be increased penalties if you target seniors in the U.S.," he says. The "former" con artist claims that his scam rarely went after the elderly, which is contrary to what investigators report happens in most of these schemes.

"Most of the people we went after were business people. There are other telephone scams that go after older people, but ours focused on those who had previously bought gems who were in their thirties, forties and fifties. They were mostly business owners, but there was an occasional retired person. No matter who it is, there are always two major factors you have to appeal to. One is their greed. If you're not greedy, then nobody can get you. And you have to appeal to their sense of urgency. They've bought hard assets, like coins or stamps or baseball cards, and when they go to sell it they're planning on screwing the tax department and they're hoping to make a profit, too. When we came along and told them they could sell their investments, they were motivated. They had an opportunity to get out."

"Yes, they got me and yes, they got the forty or so other guys, but there are three thousand guys who got away.... I think [the police] are making classic errors," he says, offering some "pointers" to investigators. "Police take their time and put together an investigation, but these telemarketing places open and close so quickly and they say, 'Well it's closed,' so they leave it alone and go on to something else. They're very slow and because they're slow a lot of guys then start up a new operation under another name. I told the authorities that. I told them that what you should do is go visit these people as soon as they start up and say, if you don't close this week, then we are going to investigate you. We'll get you eventually and here's what's going to happen, because a lot of people don't think about what's going to happen. None of the Canadians knew that in the States everybody does jail time because everybody knew in Canada that nobody gets jail time.... You scare them ahead of time. If they close down earlier, there are less victims and if there are less victims, there's less fraud."

He suggests that lighter sentences in Canada, where convicts of non-violent crimes only serve one-third of their sentence—whereas in the U.S. they are obligated to serve slightly more than three-quarters of their jail time—make setting up scams north of the 49th parallel really attractive to cons. "The odds are ninety-nine out of a hundred that if you're going to get busted in Canada, you'll end up jerking around the system and the prosecution. They'll switch prosecutors and they're overburdened because of three- and four-week trials, and so they'll make a deal with you and you end up with a fine. It's really a licence to commit fraud."

Gary Clewley, a Toronto-based lawyer who specializes in securities law, agrees. "It's a really venal crime and can be a difficult one to obtain convictions on. Telemarketers are at the bottom of the barrel. They prey on the elderly and come as close to the description of son of a bitch as I can think of. They're propelled by greed. It's one of the top five things that make people tick. If sex is number one, greed is a close second."

At the end of 1994, while the parade of fraudsters was being indicted, fallen Lutheran minister Robert Finkbeiner was convicted of defrauding US $1.4 million to invest in the gems, and was sent to jail for a year and a half.

Hartman believes that Finkbeiner's actions illustrate in the extreme how some people become so obsessed with making their money back from these schemes that they lose their sense of reality and judgment. The fraudsters "would make you feel like you had to keep your end of the bargain up, but it was simply sending good money after bad because it was already lost. In doing this Finkbeiner became so desperate that he lied in order to get the money to continue the scheme. Most people after a while begin to realize that, 'Yes, I've been ripped off. They've made promises before and didn't keep them, so I should stop.' But this guy just believed so much that they were going to cash him out that he went beyond what was reasonable to stay in the investment program."

At Michael Schaumer's and Eugene Yermus's sentencing hearing on November 8, 1995, Finkbeiner's son and two daughters asked to address the court. Paul Finkbeiner told Judge William Caldwell of the District Court for the Middle District of Pennsylvania that he wished to read a letter from his incarcerated father:

I, Robert G. Finkbeiner, am a victim of the Canadian gemstone scam. I understand that some of the men listed as owners, Mr. Yermus and Mr. Schaumer, who devised the scheme, are soon to be sentenced.... These men are directly responsible for my loss of US $1.4 million to their scam. This money represented all of my liquid assets saved up over a lifetime of honest work and monies of others from whom I borrowed at the insistence of those who worked with these men. The first monies sent to these people was in the belief that their selling and brokerage of gemstones would be profitable for me, the investor. As the scam progressed, I was not faced with the happy prospect of making money on my investment, but with the inward terror of not being able to recover my money or that of others from whom I had borrowed.

They pushed, threatened and intimidated me into believing that unless I could come up with much larger amounts of money to resolve the investment problem that I would lose all the money invested. They assured me that if I could get the money by whatever means, they could resolve the problem quickly and all would be well.... To use their words, they said "beg, borrow or steal the money" and it would be replaced in days. I thought in my terror that I had no alternative but to believe them and do as they requested. The end result is that I borrowed monies inappropriately and because of their scam am paying dearly for believing them and acquiescing to their threats and persuasion.

This has personally cost me my job as chief executive officer of a large, well-respected social service agency. It has cost me my reputation and standing in the community as well. It has also cost me my financial security since my wife and I have gone through bankruptcy.... Some of these men, I understand, have suggested that my motivation was just greed. Gentlemen, let me assure you that it was not greed at all that led me so deeply into this. Initially, there was certainly the desire to make money on their assurance of a seemingly good investment, but as I was led more deeply into this scam, it was not greed that motivated me but the utter fear and terror that I would lose other people's money and not be able to pay them back. Indeed, my worst fears have been realized, and my life inability [sic] to serve my fellow man as I have in the past has been lost.

Thanks to my faith, my family and some friends, I continue to move through this devastating time in my life. I simply ask the court to deal justly and not with leniency as it sentences these men who set out deliberately and illegally

to take other people's money and who have left a wake
of real-life victims in their path.

The Finkbeiners lost their home and the reverend's wife was
forced to move in with their youngest daughter, Amy, while her
husband was in prison. Mrs. Finkbeiner held full-time and part-
time jobs so that some of the debt could be repaid. As Amy
recalled for the court, "The time came when we all had to face
what we hoped and prayed would never happen. My mother and
my sister and I had to drive our father to prison two hours away
to drop him off. Our father approached the guard, and the three
of us stood back and watched him begin the process of his incar-
ceration. No child should ever have to see that happen to their
parent. We can honestly say that there was nothing in the world
more painful than watching that, and there is nothing anyone can
ever do or say to take that memory away."

There is no doubt that Finkbeiner was guilty of fraud. He
deceived friends and co-workers and used their money because
he became trapped in a sinkhole from which he thought he'd
never escape. But clearly the minister was no threat to society
and his family helped make restitution for the money he took.
However, his eighteen-month sentence was equal to that meted
out to some of the convicted fraudsters who were part of this
scam and others like it. Many people who look at this case shake
their heads and wonder about the obvious imbalance of justice. It
seems that even after a telemarketing operation is discovered and
fraudsters caught, the victims keep on losing, while many of the
cons continue living the good life and barely pay their debt to
society.

In addition to allowing the Finkbeiner family to address the court, Judge Caldwell gave some of the other victims an opportunity to express their feelings at the hearing. As he noted: "In addition to the letters and statements that were made today, I have received a number of other communications from people who were victims, one in particular that I recall, a woman whose son has a learning disability and who herself since this happened has been a mental patient because this money—the money she invested and hoped would grow—was to provide for his education. This is not a case where a person misappropriated funds that may have been available to him for some legitimate reason. This is a case where this money was secured from victims in the United States for the very purpose of stealing the money and depriving the owners of it."

In equally compelling testimony, the family of the elderly farmer who lost his life savings also told the court: "... Most of the men indicted in this case have supposedly liquidated their assets to pay fines and make restitution, and yet they still have homes—when some of their victims have lost theirs. They still have money to hire attorneys to represent them ... the attorneys whom they are using here today are paid for with their victims' hard-earned money. The United States government is our attorney. And although we are grateful that this case has been prosecuted, we feel a great disservice has been done to these men's victims in the plea bargains reached. A slap on the wrist is hardly a description of it....

"Michael Schaumer and Eugene Yermus can never give back to society the financial losses, the deteriorated health, the broken lives that their victims suffer, but they should pay an honest penalty. We plead with you for ourselves and the 1,900 other victims of this fraud. Please let us walk away from here today

# GREED

feeling that these men have been punished in accordance for [sic] their crimes.

"Investment is what we use to build for the future for our grandchildren and our grandchildren's education, for financial growth, for retirement. Imagine how you would feel as an investor if you were told that someone had misappropriated funds and had taken the money that you had invested. Your hard-earned money is gone. Your future had been taken away. What will you tell your family? What would you try to do to get it back? What if the telephone rang and your investment counsellor told you there was a possibility you could recover your funds? Would you try? Certainly. Most anyone would."

## POSTSCRIPT

Michael Schaumer and Eugene Yermus each received a sentence of fifty-one months and were ordered to repay Cdn $1 million in restitution to the victims. They are currently appealing their sentences. Prison terms for other convicted scam artists in this case and other related frauds ranged between eighteen and thirty-six months.

Accused fraudster Allen Grossman continues to fight extradition to the U.S. and is being represented by Toronto law firm Greenspan, Humphrey. Police allege that he has ample money to keep the litigation process rolling. Authorities say that shortly after Metropolitan Toronto Police arrested seventy telemarketers in a raid on three boiler rooms on March 5, 1993, Grossman allegedly transferred in excess of US $1 million to a Swiss bank and elsewhere. Michael Schaumer is believed to have done the same, and records show that he wired US $800,000 from his Royal Bank account in Toronto to a Swiss bank account in Zurich.

Since the U.S. uses a grid system, which outlines specific penalties for specific crimes in federal prosecutions, Judge Caldwell was constrained to handing down prescribed sentences to those in this case convicted of their charges. "It is not within my power to sentence the defendants in accordance with what the victims might want or what I might personally feel is deserving. I am confined to the range and the range is based upon the amount of money involved in losses to the victims," he said on the day of sentencing for Schaumer and Yermus. "Had the defendants not cooperated in this case I would not hesitate to sentence them at the top of the applicable range because of the egregious nature of their offences and the offences of others for whom they're responsible. Because of their cooperation, however, sentence will be imposed at the bottom of the range that applies, and if restitution is forthcoming, I would give, as I've said, further consideration to a departure."

—— 2 ——

# SMOOTH OPERATORS

T he gemstone fraudsters knew what strings to pull to get their victims to buy bogus jewels. In this case two brothers involved in the securities market pulled strings, too, but these were attached to a junior mining company's share price listed on the Vancouver Stock Exchange. For a while they were able to manipulate the stock's price to their advantage, but then the British Columbia Securities Commission stepped in and put a stop to their scheme—at least temporarily.

Eugenio and Francesco Sirianni are brothers and bear some physical resemblance to each other, but their personalities are vastly different. Eugenio, the elder, loves travelling the globe in search of investment deals, which some believe he's still doing, while Francesco is quieter and more of a family man. Better known to their friends and business associates as Eugene and

Frank, the brothers grew up in Australia after their parents emigrated to the British colony from their native Italy.

Frank is much more academically inclined than his older brother. He holds two degrees in economics and for a while lectured on accounting at Monash University in Melbourne, Australia, before moving on to manage a small computer company.

Eugene, on the other hand, is an entrepreneur. In fact, his charismatic and enthusiastic nature helped him turn many fledgling deals into successful, money-making ventures, and when Eugene took a business trip to Vancouver in the mid-'80s he was smitten with the beauty of the West Coast city and the potential to make money in its investment industry. He decided to move there to seek his fortune.

"What I saw in Vancouver was an opportunity, because the companies were somewhat smaller ... my concept was to invest in these companies myself ... and the structure of the Vancouver Stock Exchange [VSE], the methodology here, it appeared to me that there was an opportunity to make some serious money on the basis of investing in the companies that I thought were undervalued," Eugene would later tell the British Columbia Securities Commission (BCSC) about his decision to move to Vancouver. (The "smaller" companies Eugene referred to are commonly known as "small-cap" or "venture-capital" firms, which typically are young companies, such as mining operations, that are looking for investment money in order to grow.)

The VSE's roots stem back to 1907 when it opened for business as a marketplace for Canadian resource exploration companies to obtain funding for their projects. It continues to specialize in raising capital for small- and medium-sized companies, in both the resource and industrial sectors, and places fourth in

# Smooth Operators

North American trading volume after the New York, Toronto and NASDAQ (National Association of Securities Dealers, Inc.) stock exchanges. However, the VSE came under harsh criticism and closer scrutiny after tidal waves of disreputable penny-stock promoters, especially during the '60s, '70s and '80s, pounded the exchange. Millions of investor dollars were sucked out with the undertow. Regulatory authorities have since tightened the rules to clean up the VSE's image, but its sullied past still lingers.

After Eugene settled in Vancouver, he set up a business called Financial Strategy Limited, known simply as FSL. According to Eugene his firm sought investors on behalf of companies that were looking for development funds. He also put some of his own money into a few of the firms he promoted.

Eugene loved the business. He often arrived at his office at 4 a.m. in order to speak with clients around the world. He didn't mind working late or meeting business associates over dinner. Sometimes he just slept in his office when business dragged on into the wee hours. But Eugene wasn't all work and no play, he also squeezed in some leisure time. At five feet four, Eugene's Napoleonic physical stature didn't hinder his penchant for or his ability to attract tall, shapely women. During a New Year's vacation in Miami in 1989, for example, he lounged poolside with a statuesque female while he took phone calls from his brokers. Back home his sprawling office at Commerce Place, in the heart of Vancouver's business section, was not only filled with expensive trappings, it was also filled with stunningly beautiful women who, in varying degrees, were his assistants. Eugene's associates would often comment about "the view" when they came for a visit, but they weren't always referring to the mountains nearby.

Business grew quickly for Eugene. He soon had twenty

employees and also had financial interests in other businesses. He realized that he needed someone to look after his growing administrative needs while he scouted out investors for client companies. Dianne Sirianni, Eugene's now-estranged wife, suggested that he invite his brother, Frank, for a visit to see if his younger sibling would help out. Although Eugene had been busy with work and hadn't spoken to Frank for some time, he liked the idea of having someone he could trust to do the job. Frank arrived from Australia in late 1986 and, like Eugene, immediately fell in love with Vancouver. Lured, too, by his brother's promise of making some "decent money," Frank began work as FSL's office manager in early 1987. His wife and children soon followed.

From the very beginning Frank agreed to be "a second set of eyes" for Eugene, and promised to be his older brother's keeper. Things went smoothly for a while, but when stock markets crashed on October 19, 1987, the Sirianni brothers, along with the rest of the world's investment community, suffered major losses. According to the brothers, the dramatic downturn snuffed out several of their plans for deals, stock promotion and corporate financings.

After the crash, "my feeling was that the market would rebound and we would have a 50 per cent recovery within six months. Unfortunately, that happened in the principal markets, but it didn't happen in the secondary markets and that was true not only in Vancouver, but it was also true in the secondary markets around the world," Eugene said.

The "first tier" of the principal markets, or blue-chip stocks, were able to keep their heads above water after the crash, but smaller capitalized firms and individual investors, the main force behind the speculative markets, were under water for a much longer period, and many never resurfaced. The venture capital industry took a long time to recover.

With losses from the market crash continuing to put financial pressure on his company, Eugene decided to leave the "retail market" and stop promoting venture capital company stocks to investors. He streamlined his efforts and focused directly on investing his own money into companies "that had something going" for them.

However, Frank wanted to continue to seek funds from individual investors for client companies and so he created his own companies, ICL Financial Communications Inc. and Interglobe Communications Ltd. (IGC), collectively known as Interglobe, and he remained as FSL's office manager. The brothers worked side by side, with Eugene's staff at FSL and Frank's staff at Interglobe sharing office space and a common reception area. All was going well.

Then Eugene met Keith Sheedy, a stockbroker at the time with investment firm McDermid St. Lawrence. Sheedy was also the son-in-law of Lorne Camozzi, a wealthy businessman who was in construction contracting. Camozzi had financial interests in several companies, and also became chairman, founder and principal shareholder of a firm called Montreux. Montreux was registered as a resource development company and incorporated in April 1987. Eugene and Camozzi, who lived in Revelstoke, B.C., about 450 kilometres east of Vancouver, got along and began meeting over dinner to discuss business ideas. No one, except the two men, is exactly sure what they talked about, but shortly after they first met, Camozzi lent Eugene about $200,000 at an interest rate of 5 per cent per month—or a nominal rate of *60 per cent* per year. BCSC authorities later questioned Eugene about the loan, but he never revealed why he needed it.

According to records at the BCSC, it wasn't long after the loan was made that Sheedy approached Eugene to discuss his father-in-law's company, Montreux, and how Eugene could help "build investor interest" in the company. Meanwhile, Camozzi was busy making arrangements to launch the company's stock on the VSE and on July 4, 1988, Montreux's shares began trading there.

A short while after Montreux's launch at the exchange, regulatory authorities began noticing what they believed were "irregularities" in the stock's trading patterns. BCSC officials issued a stop-trading order on January 26, 1989, less than seven months after Montreux first began trading on the VSE, to investigate what was going on. During their subsequent investigation regulatory authorities also found out that Montreux was "a client" of the Sirianni brothers' companies. Eugene claimed that his primary role with Montreux was to seek "financing" or find investment funding on behalf of the company. Frank, too, acknowledged that he had a business relationship with Montreux. His company, Interglobe, charged an annual fee of $60,000 to the firm to provide "investor relations services."

After further investigation the BCSC alleged that the brothers and their companies were in some way involved with manipulating Montreux's stock prices. Following many months of delays, Eugene and Frank were finally summoned to a Commission hearing in the summer of 1990.

Eugene testified that he became involved with Montreux as a way to "ingratiate" himself with Lorne Camozzi because of the loan the businessman gave him. He admitted that he owned shares in Montreux, as did Frank, but emphatically denied that he and his brother had ever concocted a strategy to illegally manipulate Montreux's stock price.

Evidence presented by Commission staff at the hearing, and supported by David Hooper, a forensic accountant and partner at accounting firm Ernst & Young, showed that Eugene and his brother Frank had more than a passing interest in the welfare of Montreux's shares. By using a computer program developed by the VSE called Analyser, which correlates buys and sells of a stock being traded, Commission staff were able to track the price action of Montreux shares during a specific time period and, in turn, were able to connect the Sirianni brothers to those price movements.

Authorities also found out that Eugene had more than thirty accounts at over a dozen brokerage firms and that Frank had about twenty accounts at eight brokerage houses. In total, they had control over fifty trading accounts at almost two dozen brokerage firms. To put this in perspective, even the most "active" individual investors would have—*at most*—half a dozen accounts at perhaps two or three investment firms. Clearly, the trading bug was in the Sirianni brothers' blood.

Dean Holley, at the time deputy superintendent, compliance and enforcement, at the BCSC, who later became its executive director but is now a securities industry consultant, gave expert evidence at the hearing and described the trading of Montreux shares by Eugene and Frank as "pervasive."

The Analyser program helped Holley show that the Siriannis traded Montreux shares on thirty-six of the thirty-seven trading days between December 5, 1988, to January 27, 1989, and both bought and sold Montreux shares on thirty-two of those days. During this time period at least 81,700 shares were traded between the brothers' accounts through fifty-four floor trades at thirty different price and date combinations. The trades, worth about $225,000, accounted for 13 per cent of the trading volume of Montreux shares within that time-frame. On December 5, 1988, alone, the Siriannis held 412,200 Montreux shares, which represented more than 30 per cent of the company's stock. In just over a month their Montreux holdings ratcheted up to almost 40 per cent.

Holley also showed their accounts immediately before and after the trades were made during the December to January time period. He discovered that for every one of the fifty-four trades, whichever of the Sirianni brothers' accounts was "selling" Montreux shares was always in a "debit cash position" on the day prior to the sale—meaning that the account owed money. In many of the cases the sales were also made to an account that either had no money or very little cash in it. Commission staff concluded that the brokers executing the Montreux trades on behalf of the Sirianni brothers were providing them with credit or, in effect, loans. (This is legal on the part of the brokerage firms, and is similar to what a bank or trust company does for their customers. BCSC staff showed that when interest payments came due on the accounts, the Siriannis would simply shuttle the necessary funds to the broker.)

"The most viable explanation for the fifty-four trades between the accounts [held by the Siriannis] is that they were made to kite debits from one brokerage account to another in order to maintain control of a large block of shares in Montreux, which the accounts would have otherwise been unable to pay for," Holley told the hearing. Holley explained that "debit kiting" is when the buyer of a stock uses delayed settlement procedures when buying shares as a way to get credit, or money. (Under Canadian securities regulations at the time, the "settlement period" to buy a stock—when the client has to come up with the cash for his shares—was five business days from the date the trade was made. Since then the settlement period has been shortened to three business days in an effort to tighten procedures.)

Then Commission lawyer Mark Skwarok, who became the Commission's chief legal counsel but is now associate counsel with Vancouver law firm Harbottle & Co., cross-examined Eugene and asked why exchange records showed that he and his brother would typically buy Montreux shares at a higher price and sell at a lower level—making it appear that the stock was up, while Eugene and Frank seemed to perpetually "lose money" in the transactions.

Mark Skwarok: "Why did you do it?"

Eugene Sirianni: "Good question. Well as you can see, I'm selling through several houses and I'm buying through one, okay. As I mentioned to you, the trading is instigated by the broker, okay ... and the broker phones me up and says, look, you've got some credit in the account, would you like to buy something? And I'm serious, that's exactly the way it would happen."

However, Commission staff showed that the Siriannis turned the investment maxim of "buy low, sell high" into "buy *high*, sell *low*" to inflate the price of the stock so that it would be more attractive to other investors. Authorities showed that while the price of Montreux's stock moved up as the Siriannis "bought" the stock, it was pushed higher by other unsuspecting investors who believed that they were buying a "hot" stock. Meanwhile, the Sirianni brothers' holdings of Montreux shares grew in value, even though they had invested a nominal amount of their own money because they were able to secure credit from a variety of brokers. It turned into a merry-go-round of trades and loans among all the investment houses with which they dealt, and the Sirianni brothers came out on top.

In one of the more comical exchanges between the BCSC's lawyer and Eugene, Skwarok attempted to get Eugene to explain why he bought Montreux shares on December 29, 1989, at $2.90 and $2.95 per share and immediately sold them at around the same price levels.

Skwarok: "Well, it's four days after Christmas. What's your explanation this time?"

Eugene Sirianni: "I'm trying to bring everyone [his brokers] a Happy New Year" (through the commissions they would receive. A commission is the fee a stockbroker charges a client for buying or selling securities on his or her behalf).

Skwarok believed it was just another attempt by Eugene to make it appear that there was a lot of investor interest in Montreux's shares.

In a separate interview with Commission staff on June 30, 1989, Frank Sirianni admitted to occasionally trading stock for the sole purpose of transferring shares that he could not pay for and suggested his brother had done the same. Skwarok struck a raw nerve when he told Eugene at the subsequent hearing that his brother, Frank, had fingered him in debit kiting

# Smooth Operators

Montreux shares.

Mark Skwarok: "He's [Frank] suggesting you're debit kiting."

Eugene Sirianni: "Sorry?"

M.S.: "He suggested you're debit kiting. You're paying somebody to be on both sides of a transaction, or washed trading [to buy and immediately sell stock at a big profit]."

E.S.: "... No, no, no. That's not what he's saying at all. Frank's saying that instead of me buying and selling stock, okay, and paying 6 per cent [commission to a broker], I would be far better off borrowing money from someone so that I could hold onto that stock."

Obviously agitated, Eugene later returned a volley against Frank by saying that he was "astonished" when he saw Frank's trading patterns in Montreux shares. He said he was surprised by the volume of trading. Eugene told Skwarok that it was just a fluke that "some" of his trades were on the opposite side of his brother's trades. In fact, Analyser evidence showed that Eugene's and his brother's buying and selling patterns of Montreux shares were almost mirror images of each other.

Pressed further by Skwarok, Eugene attempted to explain away his investment activities by saying that he found trading "annoying" and he "did not keep close tabs" on his investment transactions. He claimed to know next to nothing about what his brother was up to, saying, "Frank and I had very little time when we were together in the office ... trading wasn't something that I was looking forward to on a day-by-day basis." He claimed that

all he wanted to do was "to help the company, to help build the company, not just simply buy stock and sell off at a high level....
I had a commitment to help the company develop to a point where it was worth a lot more," he told the hearing.

When asked why he wanted Montreux to "grow," Eugene flippantly said: "Because I'm achievement oriented." He described Montreux as originally being an undervalued company, and based his conclusion on an engineering report on the firm's aptly named "Keystone–Holy Terror Gold Mine" property. He said that even though he did not have any background in engineering, his "analytical" abilities were superior to those of Lorne Camozzi, the owner of the company.

One of the few other things Eugene acknowledged was that he opened accounts and had purchased Montreux stock on behalf of his wife (even though they had "separated" by then but continued to share the same house), their three children and his mother. He told the hearing he bought Montreux shares to preserve a future for his wife and children. "Well I don't have a [life] insurance policy even today, and I love my children very much, and I have a heart of gold for my wife as well so I set up the children's accounts with a view that I was going to trade some fairly substantial profits for them over time," he testified.

It appears that Eugene Sirianni's version of "life insurance" would provide a big payout to his family. By buying Montreux stock for his children through accounts under his wife's name he effectively became an "insider trader" because he held control over the shares. (Generally, an "insider" is described as a director or senior officer of a corporation or anyone else within the firm who may be presumed to have access to inside information concerning the company. It also includes anyone owning more than 10 per cent of the voting shares in a corporation. An insider is prohibited from making trades by using "material, non-public information." For example, in September 1996 the BCSC banned the province's former premier Bill Bennett and his brother Russell from participating in British Columbia's securities markets for ten years. The Commission charged that, as a result of a tip-off from Doman president Herb Doman, they had sold shares of Doman Industries shortly before the forest products company made an announcement that would negatively affect its share price. Doman was also banned for ten years. Russell Bennett and Doman are appealing the rulings.

What caught the Sirianni brothers, it appears, was that they perpetually failed to file insider trading reports to the BCSC. The regulatory body requires that an insider must report trades within ten days of having made the transactions. Eugene maintained under oath that he did not know that the shares in his children's accounts were considered under his control, even though he traded them.

All of Eugene Sirianni's claims—that he was too busy to keep tabs on his stock purchases and sales; that he knew little, if anything, about his brother's business; that he couldn't remember what he used the money he "borrowed" from Lorne Camozzi for; and that he rarely moved cash around to cover his tracks—simply didn't hold water. Commission staff presented compelling evidence that showed Eugene had "bought" $1.27 million worth of stock, a substantial part of which was made up of Montreux stock, and "sold" shares totalling $1.4 million—and virtually hadn't paid a dime for any of it.

"Well, I'm suggesting to you, sir, that during the relevant period, the amount of cash which flowed through your hands to the brokerage houses was virtually nil, despite the fact you purchased over a million dollars worth of stock and sold over a million," Skwarok finally told Eugene at the hearing. Eugene responded by saying that the Commission's evidence was "misleading."

The Sirianni hearing, however, was not a trial before a criminal court of law. Therefore, the BCSC staff weren't faced with having to provide proof "beyond a reasonable doubt" to win the case against the Siriannis. Like a civil case, they only needed to prove a "balance of probabilities" against the defendants.

In his final written submission to the Commission, Skwarok observed that although Frank had acted as Eugene's "eyes," the scheme had the older brother's fingerprints all over it. "Eugene was the leader and driving force in his and his brother's businesses.... His testimony was smoke, wafted about by gusts of convenience and self-interest."

And so in the fall of 1991 Douglas Hyndman, chairman of the BCSC, ruled that the Siriannis had manipulated Montreux's stock price. He wrote that the flurry of buying and selling made it appear to the public that there was a lot more investor interest in the company's shares, and that the stock "offered a much greater degree of liquidity than was actually the case." Hyndman declared that the Sirianni brothers would, in fact, pay a price for their deeds—although they were never fined.

"They didn't get a fine. Unfortunately, it's the way they ultimately were treated by the justice system," says Martin Eady, BCSC manager of investigations, compliance and enforcement, who assisted on the case. However, the primary goal of the Commission was to stop the Sirianni brothers from using the VSE as their own money-making playground.

The brothers' "pattern of behaviour was prejudicial to the public interest because it damages confidence in an open, efficient and credible securities market," Hyndman stated. In addition, their "large position in Montreux shares" financed by "very expensive credit"—the loan from Lorne Camozzi to Eugene Sirianni—gave them "a strong motive to create a misleading appearance of trading activity," and the only way they'd make any money was to "induce investor interest.... We consider it in the public interest to protect the market by removing" Eugene and Frank Sirianni "from the market and from involvement with reporting issuers for a significant period," he said.

On October 4, 1991, the Sirianni brothers were told that they would not be allowed to buy, sell or trade issues from that day forward in British Columbia securities markets for a total of fifteen years.

"A lot of people look at the Sirianni case and say, 'So what! Who did they hurt really? Eugene was very successful in manipulating the stock up. Isn't that a good thing?'" says Dean Holley today. "But we have to take action against these guys ... because if we don't, are we ever going to get people in Toronto's markets or elsewhere not to think of the VSE as the Wild West? I think we can change that mindset, but it's going to take some time."

However, Holley also cautions that "with a venture capital market, there will always be more latitude for abuse. It's inherent in the fact that you have small companies that are publicly traded. It's attractive to those people who will come and look into the window and figure a way to get that money. Over time there will be those people who will get control because there aren't enough checks and balances to enforce control.... Junior markets, venture markets are always going to be risky for two different reasons: risky because of the nature of the companies, like drilling holes in the middle of Tuktoyaktuk. The second factor is inexperienced management who are at greater risk of being morally challenged. This is a market that should only be attractive to a subset of investors."

Holley explains that the Commission is "taking a very active role in two ways: through enforcement ... trying to get people to understand what is acceptable behaviour and sanction those people who are offside. There have been something in the neighbourhood of six hundred administrative orders over the past few years. In other words, six hundred kicks at the can to get the bad guys away from the market."

## POSTSCRIPT

Eugene Sirianni was last reported "working" in Switzerland. Meanwhile, Frank's temporary immigration status expired just after the Commission's ruling against him and he returned to Australia with his family. Lorne Camozzi is retired and Keith Sheedy left the brokerage industry. Sheedy owns several properties in B.C. and now makes a living as a landlord.

# ——3——

# SEPARATING THE WHEAT

# FROM THE CHAFF

The Sirianni brothers made the Vancouver Stock Exchange their home away from home. They made the most out of their surroundings, between the grandeur of the Rockies and the Pacific Ocean. Eugene and Frank believed they had discovered a way to secure their financial futures—but they were wrong. A series of fraud cases that cropped up at the Winnipeg Commodity Exchange from the mid-'80s to early '90s also dealt with "futures." Except these futures represented legitimate goods from the earth, and it was the traders dealing with them who were bogus.

The Winnipeg Commodity Exchange (WCE) was born in 1887 in the expanse of the wide open prairies. Weathering the ravages of time, through dustbowls and droughts, world wars and shifting economies, the exchange's lowest ebb came as it neared its one hundredth birthday. In the spring of 1985 the exchange found itself mired in a scandal which led authorities to uncover a series of other frauds that shook the very foundations of the WCE. Over the next five years an army of RCMP officers and forensic accountants waded through hundreds of boxes of documents and thousands of trading-pit transactions to unravel the schemes. The investigations cost taxpayers more than $3.5 million.

The first incident involved two traders who devised an illegal trading scam in order to line their pockets with their favourite commodity—money. One trader, Gary Harpman, worked for Cargill Grain Ltd., one of the world's biggest marketers of canola, which is an improved strain of Canadian rapeseed. (Trade in canola is a multi-billion-dollar business around the globe. In recent years fat-conscious baby boomers have helped push canola's price higher by gobbling up its oil, which is known for its low-cholesterol qualities.) The second trader was Gerald Spalding, who was self-employed and traded for his own account.

Over a period of five years, Spalding and Harpman met regularly on the exchange floor. After a while, other traders became suspicious because Harpman's turf was the canola pit, while Spalding dealt almost exclusively in feed grains, and there really was no reason for them to be talking to the extent that they did. (The WCE has only two trading pits—one for oilseed contracts, such as canola, and the other for feed grains, such as oats and barley. Since 1943 Canada's wheat trading has been done through the Canadian Wheat Board, the Crown-owned central selling agency that deals only in wheat and barley intended for human consumption.)

"Harpman, who had a lot of knowledge about what Cargill

was doing, would share this information with Spalding and together they would take advantage of the price movements," says Corporal Rick Edwards, one of the investigators on the case, along with Sgt. Brian Tario, both members of the RCMP's Commercial Crime Section in Winnipeg.

The exchange "was like an old boys' club. Not a lot of people outside the industry really understood how the futures trading system worked. It was a bit of a mystery and it had its own language. There are a lot of intricacies to the industry, so a lot of people really didn't understand what to look for, or how you would be cheated," says Edwards, explaining why the scam went undetected for so long—even among experts.

Futures commodity trading can be very complex. In its simplest form, for example, there is no immediate transfer of ownership or, in the majority of cases, delivery of the actual commodity when it's traded. "In other words, you can buy and sell commodities in a futures market whether or not you own the particular commodity. In fact, most contract buyers and sellers close out their contracts prior to the delivery month so that the physical deliveries are rare, occurring in roughly only two per cent of all futures contracts," explains the Canadian Securities Course textbook. Like equity or bond traders, commodity futures traders simply execute transactions between buyers and sellers, and in futures trading it's on behalf of the contract holders, who can be individuals or companies. Commodity futures contracts are legally binding commitments to "deliver" (sell) or "take delivery of" (buy) a specific quantity and quality of a commodity at a future date and an agreed-upon price. That's why prices of commodities like orange juice can swing wildly when, for example, news of frost in Florida hits trading pits.

71

# GREED

Harpman and Spalding also used the WCE's practice to allow trades to be reported at the end of the trading session to their advantage. Procedures have since dramatically changed, but at that time they could wait the entire session, from 9:30 in the morning when it opened to 1:15 in the afternoon when it closed, to see where prices had gone. The price of any given commodity could have moved several dollars in any direction.

"What they would do is submit trades through the clearing house [where trades are processed and documented] to their own advantage, but to the detriment of Cargill Ltd.... Profits would be funnelled off to Spalding, who would kick some of the profits back to Harpman," Edwards says. The scheme "was further shrouded in secrecy because there is a lot of anonymity on the floor. A company such as Cargill might even use an independent trader to execute a trade just to hide who the trade is for, which is totally legitimate," he says.

Ray Flett, the lead prosecutor on the case and a partner at the Winnipeg law firm of Aikins, MacAulay & Thorvaldson, adds that it's "fundamental to the process that some people not be aware of what a company is doing with regard to a particular position." If they have that knowledge, he says, then "speculators can come in and drive up or down the price and have an impact on the whole process."

Because Cargill wasn't always sure who they were trading with on every deal, the company needed information that was available at the clearing house, as well as from other trading firms, in order to determine who was involved in the trades. Cargill turned to the RCMP when their own security people's attempts to investigate Harpman failed to gather enough concrete evidence. "[We] were able to identify the price, quantities and the dates for all of the trades that Spalding had executed over that five-year period. We were able to tie them right back into Cargill and we could see what profits were generated to Spalding as a result of conducting the analysis," says Edwards.

Harpman's and Spalding's "fool-proof" trading plan began to unravel when they became a little too cocky after years of success. Greed got the better of them, and they began making bigger and more frequent transactions. Their piggyness did them in.

"Spalding enjoyed uncanny success in his trades with Cargill, which always resulted in a profit to Helgera [Commodities Ltd., the company Spalding and his wife, Helen, owned] and a loss to Cargill," said Walter Folliott, the supervisor of the Grains Futures Act at the time. Flett credits Folliott, as well as Earl Basse and Charlie Foxe, two other RCMP investigators who had been looking into the Cargill matter in its early stages, with being instrumental to the ultimate success of the case. "If those guys hadn't done the work they did and hadn't given us such a strong lead to work with, then this whole thing would have gone away and nobody would have known about it. It was an amazing stroke of luck"—but not for Spalding and Harpman.

The RCMP's Edwards and Tario, and lawyers Flett and Don Bryk who, like Flett, was also hired by the federal Department of Justice to prosecute the case, still had their work cut out. Under pressure from the federal government and the exchange to get the Cargill case and others that followed resolved as quickly as possible, the men worked mind-numbing hours, seven days a week for months at a stretch. They made trips to the Chicago Board of Trade, a prime centre of commodity trading in North America, to seek the advice of experts there. "Very early on we decided Chicago was where it was going to be [to learn what they needed to know]. It's the oldest exchange around and they've been at this for a long time. We needed to ensure that the information we had was totally unbiased," says Flett.

Literally *hundreds of thousands* of trades, the majority of which were legitimate, were examined in order to pinpoint the fraudulent ones. The task prompted Edwards, Tario and RCMP computer specialists to create a computer program, still used today, that could track down "irregular trading" activities. "This case was mainly one of taking statistics and having experts comment on those statistics to tell us whether they were realistically possible, given their experience in commodities trading," Edwards says. "Basically, at that early point, no one in the RCMP had any expertise in commodities futures trading. We took commodities trading courses and options seminars. We went after whatever reading material we could find to educate ourselves so that we knew what we were talking about with some degree of proficiency."

(Cargill's case wasn't the first time allegations had been made against traders at the WCE. Incidents which occurred over several decades, a few of which dated back as far as the 1920s and 1930s, clearly showed the disdain some farmers felt towards traders and the exchange. Several farmers had even taken to calling the WCE "the house with closed shutters." Although a number of incidents were investigated by Royal Commissions, none ever sparked a criminal investigation.)

Investigators also turned to a local authority on commodities, Bob Purves, the president of the WCE from October 1988 until March 1992. "They weren't babes in the woods, but there was a lot of complicated information that had to be dealt with," says Purves, who helped in the early stages of the case.

# Separating the Wheat from the Chaff

"Spalding had traded in small-size lots in feed grains.... The fellows on the floor are always interested in what other people are doing because they try to keep the books on everybody and what their position is. They found it rather unusual that Spalding was only trading in oilseeds when Harpman was on the floor. I guess maybe they concluded that things weren't all that they should have been, so they blew the whistle on him. I give them full credit for it. They were interested in the integrity of their business," Purves says.

The RCMP were able to "match up the trades and they found that Spalding was trading back and forth with Cargill [through Harpman] and in doing that he had enormous success. At one point he had something like $109,000 in profit and zero losses," adds Flett. Since Harpman was one of several in a stable of Cargill traders, and the system made it extremely difficult to distinguish his trades from those of his co-workers, "it would have been virtually impossible to have concluded that he was doing anything wrong," Purves says. However, by turning the tables and examining trades made by Spalding, who was not part of a group of traders because he managed only his own account, police were able to find that he had accumulated profits totalling $534,300. Spalding's winning streak would have made U.S. First Lady Hillary Rodham Clinton, who's been known to dabble in commodity trading, green with envy.

"You'll find that most people do not make money on the futures market. Seven out of ten will lose money. When Spalding had a 99 per cent ratio of profits to losses, that was highly unusual. In excess of 90 per cent of his entire trading was with Cargill Ltd. That kind of solidified things with us," Edwards says. "That's like hitting the 6/49 [lottery] time after time after time. Not just once or twice. It was over and over again," adds Flett.

Purves says that the way the WCE's trade processing system was set up at the time also gave Harpman and Spalding a huge opportunity to fix trades. They were able to manipulate the data because trades were documented manually, which created delays in processing them through the clearing house. "Spalding had 20/20 hindsight. There's no doubt he made trades after the fact.... Today, it's very different, but at the time things were changing in all futures markets. Computers were not ubiquitous until the mid-'80s. Exchanges were just starting to move towards computer clearing," he says.

In addition, traders at the WCE weren't obligated to fill out order cards in ink, nor did they have to fill in every line of a card. "Right away you've got convenient ways in which trades could be made up," says Flett. "By 1985 [the year Harpman and Spalding were caught] the scope of the problem at the exchange was known. It was clear that there was a major problem here and the exchange responded very quickly. Bob Purves was instrumental in seeing that changes for the better were made. Purves is the guy who did the revision of the bylaws [that set in motion sweeping changes to improve the way in which the exchange did business]. He made tremendous contributions on the regulatory and compliance sides." Purves was also instrumental in introducing an innovative audio- and videotape surveillance system in the trading pits. The system, since adopted by other exchanges, is still there today, but is more commonly used to settle disputes over orders.

Ironically, not everyone was wildly enthusiastic about Purves's appointment as president of the exchange. Purves was criticized by some for his strong ties to prairie grain companies because he comes from a family-owned grain firm, Inter-Ocean Grain Ltd., which was started by his father in 1909. Concern over Purves stemmed from the belief that he might be inclined to give an unfair advantage to the large grain firms over smaller players. But he proved his critics wrong and ended up being a beacon of light for the exchange. "Purves is not in it for the ego trip or the salary. I think he wants to do something for the exchange," said one trader.

Purves came by his experience and values honestly. "As a youngster we used to get lectures at the dining-room table from my father about the integrity of the grain trade and that a man's word is as good as his bond," Purves says. "We heard all of the clichés about markets with integrity. But this is an industry based on integrity, and something that's impinging on that means that we have to take steps to make sure it's stopped."

Harpman and Spalding were stopped, but a major incident just before their trials almost derailed the case against Harpman. A story in the *Winnipeg Free Press* in June 1989 revealed that Spalding had pleaded guilty a half-hour before Harpman, his co-accused, had pleaded not guilty. (Spalding, who had even paid taxes on his illegal gains to help avoid detection, was given a two-year jail sentence.) After only one day into the hearing Harpman's defence counsel sought a mistrial, arguing that the story would prejudice his client's ability to obtain a fair hearing. The trial judge, Madam Justice Ruth Krindle, agreed, and set a new hearing date rather than risk having a verdict from this hearing overturned at a later date. To plug any possible information leaks from the courtroom, Judge Krindle advised all the attending lawyers at the trial to follow her example by refusing to talk to reporters outside the courtroom. "The safest thing to do when you see a reporter is say, 'Good morning,' cross the street and run like hell."

Harpman finally got his day in court on September 25, 1989, and chose to be tried before judge and jury. He probably regretted his decision because he came up against an all-women jury, and as one of them said after his trial: "He looked slick and wore expensive suits and bright blue-rimmed glasses. He wasn't a sympathetic character."

At the jury selection the prosecution looked for "older, more mature people and anybody who had a business background," but the defence challenged these candidates. As a result, they ended up with an all-female jury.

Most prosecutors in these sorts of technical cases prefer to go before a judge alone because the evidence can be extremely difficult for the average person to understand, says Flett. "If you're dealing with a judge alone, if he or she doesn't appreciate or understand the point you are making, the judge will stop and say, 'Back up a little and go through that again, I don't know what the hell you're talking about.' But if you're dealing with a jury, the jurors sit there stone-faced for the most part and you have no idea what they're thinking."

The challenge before Flett and Bryk was to get the jury to realize that, as one floor trader put it bluntly, "Even God couldn't get these trading results."

Flett decided to add a touch of drama and colour—literally—to the trial when he persuaded the RCMP investigators slated to give testimony to wear their familiar red serge tunics, spit-polished high, brown boots and beige flat-brimmed Stetsons in court. (Mounties usually only don their ceremonial uniforms for state and special occasions.) A hush fell over the courtroom when Cpl. Edwards took the stand, says Flett. "The jury was quite good and were really into the trial ... but they were especially attentive when Rick Edwards gave his testimony. He's a really good-looking guy," he says with a Cheshire grin.

Strong evidence compiled by the RCMP, not to mention the attractive way in which it was delivered, did the trick. Harpman was found guilty and sentenced to thirty months in jail. But the prosecution felt that the sentence was too light and didn't accurately reflect the depth of Harpman's deeds. Flett appealed. "The learned trial Judge [Krindle] misperceived the magnitude and complexity of the fraudulent activity and that the accused was its author," his appeal application boldly stated. Flett argued that Harpman showed no remorse and took the lead role in the scam. The appeal court ultimately agreed with Flett and Bryk and increased Harpman's sentence to four years.

Although prosecutors and police were satisfied with the trial's results, they knew Cargill's case was just the tip of the iceberg. While investigating Harpman and Spalding, the officers uncovered a series of trading irregularities at several other companies. "When we were investigating Spalding and his relationship with Harpman and analyzing their trades, we came across another trading pattern, which led into other investigations," says the RCMP's Edwards.

"We saw that Spalding also had a number of very successful trades with XCAN Grain Ltd." (XCAN is the export marketing arm for non-board grains and oilseeds for the three prairie wheat pools in Manitoba, Saskatchewan and Alberta.) Police found that Spalding had made another sweetheart deal with Gordon Cross, a futures clerk at XCAN. (Cross was not a trader; he had an administrative job which involved settling the accounts for futures trades between XCAN and its clients.)

Over a three-year period Cross skimmed a total of $30,000 from the illegal deals he made with Spalding. He received a two-year suspended sentence on the proviso that he repay the money. "Cross was an older guy who figured he was overworked and underpaid and he was looking for a little extra money on the side," says Edwards. It wasn't a massive amount, but it pointed to the strong possibility that there were others on the exchange floor who were also up to no good.

Cross testified that there were, in fact, many others making illegal deals on the side, which shocked market observers. His accusations were troubling to authorities, but they couldn't simply throw a net over the exchange in the hope of catching the bad guys. They knew that they had to take the investigation one step at a time. However, the more they looked, the more fraud they found.

When police were investigating the Cross–Spalding connection, they spotted some unusual U.S. futures trades that involved Gustave Deslauriers, the director of trading for XCAN. Deslauriers, who had ultimate say over how trades were allocated into XCAN accounts, had a profit-sharing scam going with Ross Hainstock, the head of a Vancouver-based company, Westcan Commodities Ltd. Police searched Westcan's offices and Hainstock's home and found documents that showed half of all the profits on their trades, a tidy $1.6 million, went to Westcan and a good portion of it was kicked back to Deslauriers. A third man, John Hasselaar, XCAN's chief executive officer, was also charged with accepting secret commissions.

The three men made strange bedfellows. Hasselaar was

quiet and never really comfortable with the pressures of the commodities markets. Hainstock, nicknamed "Whipper Snipper" because of the fast deals he was known to make, was very outgoing and enjoyed the good life that his under-the-table deals bought him. He loved playing host to Japanese clients who came to visit, and regularly took them out for golf on the links that backed onto his large West Vancouver home. He had a fondness for luxury cars, drove a Cadillac, and owned condominiums in Hawaii. Deslauriers, like Hainstock, worked hard and played hard, but was more "street smart." After a day of trading he enjoyed swapping stories with other traders in one of Winnipeg's better watering holes. The owner of the bar once quipped that more grain was traded there than at the Winnipeg Commodity Exchange.

The men's scheme involved many trades at a variety of exchanges, including the WCE, the Chicago Board of Trade, the Kansas City Board of Trade and the Minneapolis Grain Exchange. The fact that they used so many different exchanges made it almost impossible for investigators to nail their scam down—but they did. The trades were also done on margin, a form of leverage on the investment and commonly used in securities markets. Margin is attractive because the investor needs to put up only a portion of the total amount on the value of the investment. However, the investor must eventually pay the full amount of their purchase, even if the assets drop in price.

The daily margin requirements on the men's deals were done by XCAN through the clearing company. XCAN was then supposed to ensure that the account was properly margined (or met a minimum level of payment), but that wasn't always the case. On more than one occasion it was undermargined by more than $1 million.

Police also found that XCAN traders had taken part in what is commonly known as "circle trading," where one canola contract, for example, is traded through many trading firms and then booked back to XCAN. The practice is illegal but is a sure-fire way for traders to put money into their pockets because it generates commissions. One circle trade involved ninety-five separate transactions through a cast of dozens, and involved several firms, Casey Grain Ltd., Tradeall Brokerage Ltd., Can Am Commodities Corp. and Comex Trading Ltd.

On November 1, 1989, Hasselaar was sentenced to two years in prison and was also sued by XCAN's owners, the prairie pools, for $200,000. Two other charges against him, one of defrauding XCAN and another of conspiring to commit fraud, were dropped. Hainstock and Deslauriers were charged with two counts of fraud, but were only convicted on a margin-related offence. Deslauriers was sentenced to three years and Hainstock received two and a half years in prison.

The sentences frustrated police investigators. Clearly agitated by the sentences—after all the effort he and other investigators devoted to the case—Cpl. Edwards told a reporter at the *Manitoba Co-operator*, "We're not robots. We can't work 24 hours a day, even though we tried." Prosecutor Flett explained that the judge ruled that there had been "contrived" trades, but decided that there had been "no deceit"—a point which *must* be proven for a fraud charge to stick—because Hasselaar, XCAN's then president, knew of the arrangement. "To me that was an absolute horror story. The effort that went in on the part of everybody was enormous. It was well prepared. There was no question in my mind, although we had other disappointments along the way, not getting a conviction in that one count was a major, major disappointment," says Flett.

Another disappointment hit hard when other charges against Deslauriers, his brother-in-law, Wayne Carels, and Ken Carswell for "engaging in non-competitive trades at arranged prices" were dropped. The judge felt the accused had been denied their right to a speedy trial because it took more than three years from when the first charges were laid against them in April 1989, to a final trial date in September 1992. As a result, Flett decided to enter a stay of charges against their companies, C&D Holdings Ltd., owned by Deslauriers and Carels; WIC Investments Ltd., owned by Carels; and Casey Grain Ltd., owned by Carswell, because the only penalties against the firms would have been fines.

Undeterred, the posse of Mounties and prosecutors continued their pursuit of still other frauds. "Almost every leaf we turned over in dealing with these traders, we found someone that was up to something illegal," recalls Don Svendson, who was the inspector in charge of the Winnipeg Commercial Crime Section of the RCMP at the time of the frauds and the officer who coordinated the investigations. Svendson is now a vice-president at KPMG Investigation and Security Inc. in Toronto.

Next stop was Norm Duvell, a grain trader. He "was quite a character," says Flett. "His trading activity handled small commercial farmers' accounts." Duvell was also a major shareholder of Can Am Commodities Corp., which was run by then-president Brian Settee. Duvell had been speculating on the futures market throughout 1985 and into 1986 in a special company account. What little luck he enjoyed in his trades soon disappeared.

"As it happened, Duvell believed the market was going to go

up, so he had a series of 'long positions' [where he bought grain futures contracts in the belief that prices would move higher]. The market did the opposite, and prices went down, down, down," says Flett. As money bled from Can Am's account, Duvell still had to feed his growing margin obligations so he decided to sell his holdings at a loss. He then took "short positions" in the belief that prices would continue dropping. (A short seller is someone who doesn't actually own the commodity or stock but believes its price is going to fall. The short seller hopes to buy the security at a later date for a lower price. If the original sale is made at a price higher than the subsequent purchase, the short seller makes a profit.)

"So, he reversed himself and he managed to do that a couple of days before Chernobyl [the June 1986 nuclear disaster in the Ukraine]. Everybody thought [east European] grains were over and then [global grain] prices went way up," Flett explains.

Duvell told the RCMP that he realized he was finished when "the goddamn Russians had to blow up that atomic power plant right then.... One more day and there'd a been a hundred thousand dollars profit come back and everybody realized it was all [sic]." He said he made the trades because "you can't stop. It's just like trying to stop a crap shooter from shootin' craps."

That's when Settee took a bold and not-so-smart step. He sold carloads of grain to get the cash needed to feed Duvell's margins, which he hoped would bail out the company's growing debt. The only problem was, Settee didn't own the grain. John Boerchers and Larry Macguire, both farmers and Settee's clients, owned it. Settee only held the "ownership receipts" issued by the grain terminal, in this case in Vancouver, on their behalf. Normally, the farmers should have had the option to sell their grain whenever they wished—when they believed they'd get the best price for it. However, without their permission, Settee sold five carloads of rapeseed and one of flax for more than $170,000.

Macguire testified in court that he not only lost the money from the grain sale, but also lost $21,000 because a cheque from an earlier sale bounced. Another $19,000 was lost when Can Am defaulted because of nonpayment of a margin account.

"The process of ownership of the grain is unbelievable. From the time the guy puts the grain into the car and it gets put onto a boat [for shipping to other countries], it's controlled by a variety of documents. In effect, the warehouse receipts were the documents that Settee used without the authority of the farmers. The farmers trusted the guy and figured he'd do what he was supposed to do, which was to phone them for authorization. Settee never did that," Flett says.

At his trial Settee claimed that selling the farmers' grain without their authorization, but with a commitment to pay the cash back later, was commonplace within the industry. "It was reasonable as long as we're an ongoing operation. We never saw any problem with selling grain on hand as any other corporation did," he said. He also said it wasn't out of the ordinary for grain to be sold and then the proceeds deposited to a general operating fund, as happened in this case. When the farmer wanted to sell his grain, the broker would calculate the profits according to the market prices on the day of the request and issue a cheque, said Settee. "Our intention would be to make the settlement with the farmer when we received instructions at market value," he said.

But his and Duvell's desperate actions backfired. They were never able to get their account back on the right side of the market in 1986. Chernobyl's nuclear disaster eventually reached halfway around the world and snuffed out Can Am, too.

Settee eventually pleaded guilty to defrauding Can Am, and although he claimed innocence to seven counts of grain theft he was found guilty on all charges. On February 6, 1990, he was sentenced to three and a half years in prison. On June 24, 1992, Duvell was also sentenced to three and a half years for defrauding Can Am by trading in futures contracts through Can Am without posting any margin money.

Of all the fraud cases that rocked the Winnipeg Commodities Exchange, this one was shrouded in ambiguity. Was this really a fraud? Certainly, greed and ego didn't seem to be factors. Settee was particularly well liked and respected in the grain-trading community and some felt he was just trying to keep his company afloat while he worked out Duvell's trading losses. In fact, former WCE president Bob Purves believes that Settee's actions might not have been the most prudent, but they weren't deliberately illegal. He feels Settee didn't deserve a prison sentence. "Quite frankly, I think Settee was so shattered and so distraught that he just went to pieces and said it was all his fault," says Purves.

"All of this came crashing down because of Chernobyl, so the company failed and the whole thing collapsed.... My own view is that this should have been regarded as a commercial failure, a bankruptcy. It was really stretching things to say that it was fraud. Nobody intended this result. It wasn't sort of a scheming thing, it just happened. Now the exchange has a rule that requires segregated funds and that customers' money cannot be used to margin positions of the company," says Purves.

On the other hand, prosecutor Flett is steadfast in his belief that Settee was "part and parcel" of the deal and knew full well what Duvell was doing.

Looking back over the frauds, Purves admits that the Cargill and XCAN scams, in particular, were a blow to the exchange. He feels that some of the media coverage of the frauds was unwarranted and negative towards the WCE. The exchange got "a bum rap," he says. But he's quick to point out that the thefts occurred *within* the companies' trading accounts and that the fraudsters abused the WCE in order to make illegal trades. He is proud, however, that the exchange and its reputable traders fought back and improved trading standards. "What did the trade do? Why, they rolled up their sleeves and undertook a series of changes," says Purves. He says the exchange now meets international standards and it's going to stay that way.

There is no doubt that Purves set the tone for the WCE's future and the people who followed in his footsteps. In 1992 he handed the torch to former Mountie Fred Siemens to carry on the job as president. Like Purves, Siemens's experience in the grain trade was ideal for the job. He was appointed director of compliance at the WCE in January 1992, and had already spent two decades in the RCMP. Siemens was the first officer to take a look at the problems at the WCE and "set the pattern for all the investigations. All police knew was that they had an enormous problem and Fred sorted it out," Flett says.

Siemens's honest approach and straightforward manner went down well with the floor traders and he gained their confidence in no time. "I believe very strongly in a market economy. Supply and demand in anything, be it a good like a commodity that we trade, or be it labour, you'll find its true value.... The WCE is the last bastion of the true open-market environment in its purest form," says Siemens.

# GREED

Like Purves, Siemens still bristles at the way in which he believes the media reported the WCE-related fraud cases as they unfolded. "The fraudulent aspect and seemingly large sums of money became very readable. The exchange was under attack from every forum. But the majority of transactions that resulted in court action were properly executed trades on the trading floor, and then taken into a back office and the companies were the victims. Admittedly, the trading systems were abused, but for the local press that was seemingly immaterial."

He feels the exchange was vindicated when a government-appointed committee, the Western Grain Marketing Panel, which was made up of representatives from both public and private backgrounds, recently concluded that the exchange had taken appropriate steps to restore public confidence. The panel gave it a "glowing report. This is a place of integrity where prices are discovered openly and efficiently," says Siemens emphatically. (After accomplishing so much and helping the WCE get back on track, Siemens decided to pursue other business interests in Alberta and left the exchange in the fall of 1996.) To the investigators, prosecutors and representatives of the WCE, there's relief that the ordeal is over and pride in the knowledge that the market they helped restore continues to thrive.

But Bob Purves says participants in investment markets, from traders to regulators, cannot rest on their oars and must work hard to ensure integrity and confidence in all capital markets. "One way to make sure it doesn't happen is to make everybody understand fraud is not acceptable," adds Purves. Although he recognizes it will never be a perfect world, he tells the story of his meeting with Ben Gunn, then in charge of World Commodity Market Surveillance at the Bank of England, and Gunn's pragmatic approach in dealing with fraud. "I had visited with Mr. Gunn each time I went to London for several years. In 1986, shortly after it became apparent that some members of the Winnipeg Exchange had been involved in fraudulent activity, I told him of my deep disappointment at those members who had committed fraud at the institution that I regarded so highly. His advice was helpful and interesting. He said, 'Markets are places where money changes hands. They always attract individuals who want more to stick to their jeans than is proper. Markets must have proper rules, and enforce those rules through effective surveillance. When fraud is discovered, root out those involved, deal with them, and get on with operating the market.' "

# 4

## PENNIES FOR

## THEIR STOCKS

Making it or breaking it in the markets depends a great deal on how much you know about what you're getting into. As seen at the Winnipeg Commodity Exchange, all of the fraudsters were expert traders who manipulated the rules of the game. The "unbeatable" winning streak enjoyed by two of the traders ended when their slippery canola oil deals were finally reported, and that led to the discovery of other scams. Unlike these "professionals," many investing in the market are neophytes. But the markets, just like the jungle, have members who prey on the weak and enjoy going in for the kill.

Judith Marcella Switzer Manning was a shrewd businesswoman in an industry and an era dominated by men. Coincidentally, it was through the two most important men in her life, her father, Horace Switzer, and her husband, Ted Manning, that she learned

93

about the investment industry—at least, their version of it.

Born a year after the stock market crash of 1929, Judith grew up in comfortable surroundings during a time when many people were barely able to scrape by. As a young girl in the '40s she attended Toronto's Loretto Abbey, a Catholic private school, and, although a Protestant, she was president of the school's Catholic Truth Society for a time. The irony that she held such a position hasn't been lost on some who know her now.

Had it not been for a turn of events—among them, the early death of her mother in 1952—Judith might have followed a more traditional path, one that most of her friends and contemporaries walked: marriage, children and becoming a housewife. After a brief spell in New York she returned to Toronto and went on to marry and have children, but the houses she loved most and thrived in were investment houses. First, it was her father's, Cardigan Securities Ltd., and eventually, her husband's, E.A. Manning Limited. She relished her work and excelled at it.

Both Judith's father's and her husband's companies were broker-dealers. Unlike full-service brokerage firms, which typically offer an array of investment services to both retail and institutional clients, the original broker-dealers financed highly speculative ventures and would then sell the related securities, usually in the form of penny stocks, to individual investors. Penny stocks are low-priced issues which begin selling at less than a dollar per share. Today, broker-dealers rarely, if ever, put up venture capital, the seed money that neophyte companies need to get established. The vast majority of broker-dealers now focus on promoting and selling penny stocks.

When Judith met her future husband in her dad's office, she was a lanky, attractive thirteen-year-old who was attempting to persuade her father to buy her a twenty-five-dollar dress for a special dance. It was a lot of money during the lean war years of the early '40s. Ted Manning, who at the time was visiting Horace Switzer, apparently offered to buy the dress for Judith, reportedly telling Horace: "If you don't buy it for the kid, I will." Judith got the dress.

Some years later, in 1954, she married her benefactor.

Not only was there a twenty-eight-year age gap between Judith and Ted, their social backgrounds were worlds apart. Judith's patrician upbringing in Toronto afforded her private schools and pretty clothes, whereas Ted's childhood could best be described as Spartan. He was a Barnardo Boy, raised in one of Ireland's Barnardo orphanages, but he overcame the challenges of an impoverished upbringing and emigrated to Canada in 1919. Soon after their marriage they started having children: Ted Jr., Judy and Marty. After the death of Judith's mother, they took in Tony, a boy who had been adopted as a baby by Judith's parents.

Judith helped her husband with his business as much as she could while raising their children, but when Ted became ill with prostate cancer in 1962, her responsibilities increased. Finally, in 1979, at the age of seventy-seven, Ted succumbed to what had developed by then into bone cancer. Over the years, Judith had tended to her children and her husband's business, and upon Ted's passing took on running the firm with all the energy she could muster. It turned out that Judith Manning was highly energetic.

In a very flattering article in the April 1987 issue of *Canadian Business*, writer Mike Macbeth lauded Judith as a guardian of integrity within the broker-dealer community at the time. "Broker-dealer. The name alone evokes memories of the sleazy boiler rooms and bucket shops of the '50s and '60s that were renowned for selling worthless mining stock to a gullible public. ... Broker-dealers—the illegitimate cousins of traditional stock-brokers. But Canada's top broker-dealer could not be more legitimate. In fact, Judith Manning, the 57-year-old president of E.A. Manning Ltd. of Toronto and the only woman on Bay Street [sic], is leading a drive to clean up the $30-million business," the feature on Judith enthused.

Broker-dealers actually originated more than sixty years ago when mining prospectors needed money to finance their operations. Turned down by the banks because of the highly speculative nature of their businesses, they looked to broker-dealers for help. The broker-dealers would put up money at a premium and then sell shares of the mining property to people over the phone, most often using aggressive, sometimes belligerent selling tactics. Their tarnished reputations grew in notoriety as the public learned that many of the operations were run by charlatans who duped investors into buying worthless stocks. Usually, investors weren't told or didn't realize that the broker-dealer owned all or most of the stock, and that the low-cost securities weren't even listed on an exchange. Unless the mine turned a profit, or, as it evolved over the years to include just about any other kind of highly speculative venture-capital business, the shares had no value. Either way, the broker-dealers made money and would then move on to the next deal.

"The Windfall scandal of 1964 thoroughly confirmed the highly speculative nature of mining stocks: a Royal Commission found instances of illegal insider trading by Windfall Oils & Mines Ltd., a small Toronto-based mining exploration company. After Windfall, the OSC [Ontario Securities Commission] tightened the regulations enough to squeeze out all but the most aggressive, efficient or lucky promoters and broker-dealers," Macbeth wrote. During the late '70s and early '80s a nine-member broker-dealer cartel of sorts was formed to create the Broker-Dealers Association of Ontario, "a self-regulating body that had a reputation for being blatantly self-serving," the article stated.

Judith eventually resigned from the Broker-Dealers Association, which soon disbanded anyway because of growing dissension among its members. She then registered her company as a securities dealer, and a handful of other broker-dealers followed her lead. But as regulatory authorities turned up the heat, several remaining broker-dealers decided to shut down.

As a securities dealer, E.A. Manning could sell stock through other, full-service brokerage houses, and market securities such as mutual funds, but it didn't own a seat on an exchange. OSC staff had long suspected that Manning was a "boiler room," as Macbeth's article described other broker-dealers.

"We suspected that they were operating a boiler room and we set out to investigate whether, in fact, this was the case. In order to do this, we had to peel back the veneer of a legitimate brokerage firm and get to the core, which we suspected was rotten," says Mark Gordon, senior legal counsel of the Enforcement Branch of the OSC.

Gordon, whose well-known zeal for his work earned him the nickname "Eliot Ness" after the U.S. Federal Treasury agent who made a mission out of dogging gangsters like Al Capone during the Prohibition of the '20s, teamed up with Brian Butler, a senior forensic accountant of the OSC's Enforcement Branch, to investigate what was really happening at Manning. Interviews with former Manning salespeople and clients confirmed their suspicions.

Gordon and Butler were told that Manning used a three-tiered telephone sales force divided up into "qualifiers," "openers," and "loaders"—exactly the way in which boiler rooms traditionally operated. The task for Manning's qualifiers was simply to make cold calls to people, whose names were generally plucked from the phone book, and secure them as leads for the next level of sales force. Qualifiers, who were generally not registered with the OSC, were expected to make about two hundred calls a day and, reading from a prepared script, ask the prospect whether he or she wanted to receive the Manning newsletter. If the prospect agreed, the person would be told that there would be a follow-up call from a salesperson within a couple of months if a good investment opportunity came along—which, of course, was usually the case. This was sometimes referred to as "baiting the hook." If the prospect didn't object to this, they would then be considered a "lead" and their name would be marked on a card with all of their pertinent information, and passed on to an opener.

The newsletter, which prospects would receive from the qualifier shortly after being contacted, had the look of a polished, informative publication. Its content suggested that Manning had a research department, with full-time research analysts at their disposal. In fact, Manning didn't have analysts on staff. The newsletter offered tidbits about the economy and market information, and gave the impression that Manning was a full-service investment house, rather than an outfit essentially only selling penny stocks from its inventory.

A few weeks after the contact made by the qualifier, an opener would call the prospect to "set the hook"—or make an initial sale of one of Manning's products, also known in the industry as the "house" stock. Openers were trained to use extremely high-pressure sales tactics, and told that they shouldn't be concerned about the client's financial needs or circumstances. The most valuable sales technique, openers were told, was to tell the prospect that they were being offered an incredible investment opportunity and that they shouldn't pass it up. Openers were trained to appeal to a person's ego and desire to make money, and would suggest to the prospect that he was a highly desirable client. Manning's openers knew how to press the greed button, and, indeed received considerable training in this regard from the chief loader and trainer, Doug Elik. Prospects were told that they would be well looked after and that the relationship with the opener would be financially fulfilling and long-term. In fact, after the opener made the initial sale, in virtually every case he would no longer have any contact with the client. The next level of "salesman" would then take over.

Openers were taught never to take "No" for an answer, and were only to obliquely imply that the investment involved some risk. They played up the virtual certainty of big profits within a short period of time, and would slip in the point that the sale was a "principal" one, or a sale from Manning's inventory. A lot of people weren't exactly sure what that meant until it was too late. Unfortunately, it meant that most clients would rarely, if ever, be able to unload their shares because there was no "open market" in which to sell them. Another favourite approach Manning openers used was to convey a sense of urgency and bully the prospect into buying a stock right away. Prospects were told the stock's price was about to move higher and that they only had a narrow window of time to buy it. Openers would push the fear button—the fear of missing out on a great opportunity to make money.

Usually, openers would begin pitching stocks at fairly lofty purchase levels, starting as high as five thousand shares, then work their way down to as low as two hundred shares, if necessary. The whole point was to get a prospect on board as a client. The higher initial recommendation level was used to give openers room to negotiate down and persuade the prospect to buy some stock. Once a potential customer bit, the opener had done his job. He was also rewarded well for his work. Manning would pay a $17\frac{1}{2}$ per cent commission of the total cost of the shares sold to the customer, providing the client didn't sell the stock within ninety days. Considering that at most full-service investment company brokers receive commissions of between 2 and 3 per cent, Manning openers were given generous pickings. However, if the client sold early—which was difficult for them to do at the best of times since they were usually dissuaded from doing so— Manning would claw back the commission paid to the opener. The payback clause kept sales staff highly motivated to keep clients on the hook.

OSC staff were told that after the opener had done his job, the client's file would be passed on to Judith Manning, who would select a loader to whom the file would go next. Loaders served two purposes: first, to get the client to buy as much stock as possible, and second, with the exception of getting the client to switch from one Manning house stock to another, to ensure that the client didn't sell his or her shares. Since, for practical purposes, Manning would be the only buyer on a resale, Manning had every reason to discourage resales.

"Manning was selling highly speculative penny stocks using an intensive telephone sales campaign by its sales force. Investors would be set up with a small amount of stock by the opener, and then loaders would follow up with a knockout punch and load them up with a much larger amount of stock," says Gordon. "Once Manning got out of the deal, which usually took three to six months, the stock would almost always return to its pre-Manning sales campaign value, virtually pennies. Some investors lost their life savings, others, a thousand dollars, but to them it was a lot of money....

"This investigation pulled at your heartstrings. We interviewed investors from all over Ontario and from all walks of life. It made our conviction stronger. After we met with some of them, we said, 'This has got to stop.' We had time on our side and we just kept plugging away. We were on the side of the angels and, in the end, we were successful. The decision speaks for itself," Gordon says.

On November 6, 1995, the OSC announced that it had cancelled Manning's licence and that it was also banning for life from the investment industry Judith Manning and her children, Ted Jr. and Marty, along with Elik, who was treated as a surrogate child by Judith. Some observers felt Manning's move to file for bankruptcy one month before the Commission's ruling was a ploy to escape criminal investigation, and/or civil litigation from former investors. Judith Manning and Elik also filed for personal bankruptcy.

"From the evidence, it is clear to us that Manning never intended to permit its customers to make a profit, and there was no evidence before us that it did," the OSC said in its ruling. The Commission also observed that the broker-dealer "failed to display common decency towards their clients." At the time, Judith Manning called the decision "one-sided" and *The Financial Post* reported that she said, "We knew that the cards were stacked against us from the beginning."

Clearly, the Commission agreed with Gordon and Butler that Manning was indeed operating a boiler room.

"The nagging part is that we registered these people," says Larry Waite, director of the OSC's Enforcement Branch. "Our job is never done, but we feel we had significant success in this case."

Despite Judith's claims in the April 1987 *Canadian Business* article that, "In the beginning I didn't know anyone in the business, and it is a male-oriented business—it was hard for me to hire salespeople. I had to train my own, to have higher ethics, to sell with integrity and full disclosure," sworn testimony by former employees and victims of Manning is in sharp contrast to what she and her company made themselves out to be.

Key testimony at the company's OSC hearing in September 1995 came from a young man, Krikor Ghanaghounian, who had been hired by Manning in August 1993. Fresh out of university and armed with a brand new bachelor's degree in business administration, Ghanaghounian had hoped to learn the investment industry's ropes at a smaller firm. He figured E.A. Manning Limited would be as good as any.

He started out at Manning as a qualifier. His indoctrination included being handed a list of professions of people he "was not to contact" because they would be inclined to ask too many questions. The list included lawyers, judges, dentists, doctors, police and bankers. In one instance a lead he provided was rejected because the person indicated he was a newspaper reporter.

Ghanaghounian was also told to be careful when dealing with women because, as one opener told him, "They ask too many questions, and bitch too much when they lose money."

As with other qualifiers at the company, all of the people Ghanaghounian contacted were randomly selected through the phone book, but he soon stumbled upon some angry former Manning customers. Ghanaghounian became concerned when he heard them describe almost identical stories about the way in which they had been treated by the company's sales staff. "Some of these individuals had bought a stock which initially rose in value, but when they tried to sell they were told that their broker was not available, or had quit. These customers felt that they had been deliberately avoided by Manning. When they were able to reach a salesperson, the salesperson either sold the stock at a loss or tried to convince them not to sell it."

Ghanaghounian had read an article in *The Financial Post* indicating that the OSC had been looking into questionable practices at Manning. "I was confused. I thought if I went to the Commission it would just be a repeat of what they already knew. It's an indication of how green I was," Ghanaghounian says today. Nonetheless, he decided to call the OSC and went to their offices at Queen and Bay streets in downtown Toronto to "tell them about my experiences."

Although Ghanaghounian's assistance proved very helpful in the case against Manning, OSC staff were careful to advise him that it would be his decision alone to continue working at the broker-dealer, as well as his decision to supply behind-the-scenes information about Manning's operations. They told Ghanaghounian that since he had completed the Canadian Securities Course and sales exam, he was "aware of the requirements of registered representatives." One of the primary edicts of the Canadian Securities Course is the "Know Your Client Rule," which stipulates that a broker must have a clear understanding of his or her client's financial situation, risk tolerance, income requirements, preference of investments and time horizon. Under no circumstances is a registered broker allowed to recommend unsuitable securities and, of course, a broker is never allowed to lie to a client.

Ghanaghounian left Manning briefly in the fall of 1993 to begin work on a master's degree and then in December called the company to see if he could return to begin training as a salesman. Although he had previously worked as a qualifier, he did not know how brokers were trained because Manning kept the qualifiers and sales staff in separate locations. He also felt that if what he had been reading about Manning was true, he had the option to leave.

On January 4, 1994, Ghanaghounian started the New Year at the side of a phalanx of Manning openers, or their version of junior brokers. He was told about a stock they were selling to clients that day. What he wasn't immediately privy to was that every three to six months certain "new" stocks would be promoted following the rise and, eventually, demise of the stocks the sales staff had just been selling. In fact, OSC staff evidence ultimately showed many of the stocks sold by Manning had remarkably similar trading patterns. It didn't appear to matter what kind of industry the stock's company was in, or the products and services sold. Although some of the penny stocks were "listed" in the newspapers, which a number of investors interpreted to mean that they were being actively traded on an exchange, most were traded in the Over-the-Counter (OTC) market, whose origins were from a time when securities were traded over the office counters at investment firms. The OTC market is also known as the *unlisted* market. The majority of stocks offered by Manning—although they represented shares in real companies—were never traded on an exchange.

Evidence at the OSC hearing revealed that Manning "effectively controlled" the market of the stock it was promoting, either alone or sometimes with another penny-stock dealer. Some would even say Manning was the market.

Since Manning generally owned the stock, it could determine the price at which it was willing to sell the stock. New price settings would simply be shouted across salesmen's desks by Elik or Ted Jr. when a price change was deemed necessary and, in turn, the sales staff would inform clients. Typically, a stock would start off at around 30 to 40 cents. While openers sold the stock to new clients it would climb quickly, usually within a few weeks, to as high as $1.30 to $1.90, or more. As the price rose, investors would be pushed to buy and the loaders would step in to load up the clients with as much stock as they could get them to buy. The stock would then tend to plateau for a while, regardless of how many more people invested in it. At this point the end of the stock's life was near, and then, with few exceptions, it would drop like a rock. As soon as Manning was finished with a sales campaign, or "off the deal," as it was known, the stock would plummet. Profits were almost always realized, not by the investors, but by Manning, its management and sales staff. Investors were left holding the bag, usually an empty one. Elik, in fact, told trainees that "90 per cent of clients would lose, but we would make money."

Ghanaghounian's early training consisted of sitting next to

openers and listening in on conversations they had with prospective clients, people whose names and basic information had been supplied by the qualifiers. Ghanaghounian, who was an efficient note-taker as a result of his university training, wrote reams of "sales tips" and information on the Manning approach to dealing with customers. Ironically, it was Manning's staff who encouraged Ghanaghounian to write down everything he was taught, and it was his meticulous notes that helped sink Manning.

"As part of our training, Doug Elik [Manning's top loader] suggested that we call [CIBC] Wood Gundy and other similar dealers and pretend we are a 'lay down.' That is, we should call up and say we just inherited $50,000 and are looking to invest and see what they say," Ghanaghounian said. "Doug said to listen to what these [brokers] said and that this is not what he wanted us to be like, and that if we were a follower of one of these brokers, we would not be successful." Ghanaghounian and other neophyte sales staff called investment advisers at Nesbitt Burns, Midland Walwyn, Scotia McLeod, and RBC Dominion Securities. "None of the salespersons we talked to would sell us any stocks over the phone. They each said they needed to know more about us and some wanted to meet in this regard, while others wanted to send us some introductory information," he said.

Ghanaghounian noted that Elik told his "students" that these kinds of brokers had no place at Manning and the fact that they wanted to send out more information was "bullshit." "Doug said, 'It's like the Wild Kingdom, when the shark smells blood, they move in for the kill and that's what this is.' "

According to Ghanaghounian's work diary he was also told that openers were expected to "give two strokes and then ask for money" when dealing with prospective clients. "A 'stroke' was something about the company or myself," Ghanaghounian explains, and he was told to "just keep asking for money." Ghanaghounian soon learned that the opener's primary objective was to get money in the door. He was taught that it really didn't matter what the name of the stock was, or what kind of company the shares represented—whatever was being flogged by Manning that day was the stock of choice.

If an opener was turned down by a prospect—usually, this would have been after a lengthy struggle over the phone—the opener would sometimes suggest to the prospect that they should monitor the penny stock's price in the newspaper to see if the recommendation to buy was right. Of course, since Manning owned the stock outright and set its price, not surprisingly the price would move higher. It would then be time for the opener to call the prospective client again and hype up the opportunity to get in on the action. Openers were taught by Elik and Ted Jr. to "battle" with the clients until they handed over their money—that was their only goal.

Ghanaghounian also learned that openers were supposed to use "action words" like "take" and "grab" in their pitch. He was told never to ask a prospect, "Do you want to *buy* some stock?" Rather, he was supposed to tell them, "Let's *grab* or *take* some stock for you." The tactic was to help camouflage the fact that there was money involved in the transaction. Openers were also expected to talk excitedly, but at the same time in a vague way with few details, about a penny stock's potential. It was all to get the client to buy some stock without knowing for sure what they were getting. Tactics included referring to Manning's in-house research department, which they didn't have. Another was to reassure the prospect that there was little risk involved in buying highly speculative securities.

One of the most widely used sales techniques was for the salesperson to hint that he was in possession of inside information about the company whose stock he was promoting. This could be in the form of a pending announcement, or simply some good news about the company. Sales staff would also use positive and accurate information about a large, blue-chip corporation, usually a natural resource firm like a mining operation, and in some way tie that company's good news back to the totally unrelated penny stock's company. In fact, securities regulations preclude brokers from telling clients that they have inside information. Whether the information be true or false, what is known as "tipping" a client with inside information is illegal.

During his first day of sales training, Ghanaghounian met opener Jamie Wilkinson, his third "tutor" of the day. During one of his conversations with a client, Wilkinson simultaneously wrote some notes and handed them to Ghanaghounian. They read: "JAMIE'S CHEESY (BUT EFFECTIVE) TIPS ON SELLING STOCK: It's not what you say, it's how you say it; Don't talk about the stock, talk about yourself; Appeal to greed, sensibility and rely on confidence." Ghanaghounian remembers that Wilkinson also told one customer, who "I assumed had lost money on mining shares previously purchased through Manning and was unhappy," that "I'm an older guy, more conservative. I deal with industrial companies." Ghanaghounian figured Wilkinson looked to be only "in his twenties." According to Ghanaghounian, Wilkinson also told the client, "There are rumours of a reorganization of the mining company within the next six months." After continuing to pitch the stock to the client, "Jamie then told the customer that the 'trade's already gone through' [meaning

Wilkinson had already committed the client to the purchase]. After the conversation ended, I asked Jamie what he meant by the phrase and he responded, 'I lied.' "

Manning had thousands of clients, many of whom resided outside Toronto in small communities throughout southern and northern Ontario. However, one of these victims, like Ghanaghounian, also helped the OSC's case against the broker-dealer. She was an exception to the Manning practice of avoiding females as clients, but she had something too tantalizing for loader Doug Elik to pass up: money and gullibility. The woman lives in a small community and says her home life and health, almost destroyed because of her ordeal with Manning, still aren't the same. She has not yet been able to tell her family that she had invested and lost the $50,000 they gave her as a gift, which was supposed to go towards building a house. Although she told her husband about the losses, she asked that she remain anonymous for purposes of recounting her story.

"It's an embarrassment. This was money that was provided to me by the family and I'd really prefer that they not know what I did with the $50,000. It would just break their hearts.... I'd probably borrow before I would tell them. It was through my mother's hard work, and I couldn't bear to tell her that I lost it. I thought that as long as I knew what was going on, I'd just sell [my stocks]. But I couldn't, [Manning salespeople] wouldn't allow it. It was terrible.

"They phoned me and told me about these stocks, Rocklite and Rusty Lake. I remember at the time I didn't feel totally comfortable, but I believed this was a legitimate broker. I just wanted to build on my money, but [Manning staff] never mentioned it was speculative. You know, some people might say I'm greedy, but I don't consider myself to be greedy. I think the people at Manning were greedy. I couldn't sleep at night if I did this to people. They don't think twice about it. They knew that this was money that was very important to me. They make it seem like they have your best interests at heart, which is what a stock-broker should do. The thing is they didn't pressure a lot initially and I bought $1,000 [worth of stock]. But then Doug Elik came into my life and that was when my whole life changed for the worse. I never received any papers from them to state anything about how speculative these stocks were, and they're supposed to send this information. I am stupid for falling for people like them, but I always believed that other people are like what I'm like. I would never do that and I would never assume that people would do that. I'm shattered and I don't believe in anyone any more."

She continues: "I bought the stock [Rocklite] in 1993 and I was told it would trade on the Toronto Stock Exchange. I'm isolated here and I don't get *The Globe and Mail* and the local paper didn't carry the information. They never said otherwise and at first I didn't think it would go as well as it did—for the stock to double and triple and so on. I later learned that was something they programmed it to do.

"When Mr. Elik knew that he bled me out of everything, I got a call from another [salesman] and he was trying to get me to borrow the money. He told me that I would be able to pay the money back in three months. It just continued on and on. Even when Doug Elik left the scene he gave me to someone else. Mr. Elik was abusive with me when I asked to sell my stock. He would first tell me, 'I promise you that it won't go below what you paid. I promise you that won't happen.' He'd then tell me,

# Pennies for Their Stocks

'You better get [the money] to me now, I've got inside information. I'll hold it for you because I know you have to go to the bank.' It was very high pressure.

"I didn't even know that there was [the Ontario] Securities Commission until I went to see my accountant. Now I don't even own legitimate stocks. I can't trust anyone. I wouldn't care if it was [a blue-chip stock like] General Motors, I can't bring myself to buy it. It's like I gave it to Mr. Elik and he ran off with it. I may as well have just given him the cash. Everything was just numbers after a while—you'd write a cheque for $13,000—it wasn't like I was holding the actual cash," she laments.

After countless attempts to get Elik to sell her holdings at *any price*—with no success—it took the woman another three months before she was able to get hold of Judith Manning to complain. Whenever she called the firm she was told that Judith was either in meetings, out of town or just not available to talk. Judith Manning finally called and informed the woman that the firm's stockbrokers worked for the company and not the client. "It was a totally different vision of what I had of a stockbroker. I believe a stockbroker is someone who works for me, someone who's a professional who advises me about what to do and works for my best interests. If I were to do things that they did, I'd be out of a job [as a professional in education]. If I did something against a student I'd be answerable to a governing board. There are people who check up on me. I assumed that not only were they professional but that they have to do things legally. This is Canada." She was incredulous that this kind of conduct could happen in Canada, and she thought the police or the government would protect her from it. In fact, that's exactly what the OSC was trying to do, but unfortunately, help came too late.

"It was very frightening for these people. Even coming up to the hearing, some of them thought they were responsible for the loss. They felt they were the cause of the problem and were embarrassed to report it," says Butler.

"The biggest regret of this investigation is many of the novice investors lost money and may never invest in the stock market again," observes Butler. "If they go to legitimate firms and get proper investment advice they would probably, over the long term, make money."

Butler says one of the challenges the OSC and other regulatory agencies like it face "is that no one ever calls up the Commission and complains when they make money. This is an industry where people will make money and people will lose money and some-times when they lose money they think it's as a result of some improper activity on the part of the registrant. But in this [Manning] case, they were right. There was improper activity."

But to prove that it was illegal activity, and despite former Manning employee Ghanaghounian's solid testimony, they needed airtight evidence. OSC staff had corroborating statements from several other former Manning salespeople and former clients, but luck was on the OSC's side when they received a phone call from yet another Manning victim, Doug Webb.

Webb, in his late forties and living in Guelph, a city about sev-enty-five kilometres west of Toronto, first contacted the OSC to find out what kind of reputation Manning had and how he could go about filing a complaint against the brokerage firm. During conversations with Webb, Commission staff learned that he had been battling multiple sclerosis for more than two decades and was on a government disability pension of less than $9,000 a year. When they heard that Webb made a habit of taping all of his conversations, both personal and business, because his affliction made it virtually impossible for him to write down important dates and information, they knew they had Manning in the bag.

According to Webb, he was first contacted by Michael McCart, a Manning opener on August 13, 1992. "On August 17 [McCart] phones back after having sent the information [on a stock called Murbank]" and told Webb that he thought this stock was a "really good deal." Webb sent his first $1,000 to cover the cost of his purchase. "We're talking $1,000. We're not talking about any really serious amount of money," Webb says of his initial investment. Confined to a wheelchair and living alone since both his parents died several years ago, Webb felt the investment might give him something to focus on and would help him build a bigger nest egg. He sought advice from his brother-in-law "right at the very beginning. He is in business and he said, 'Why don't you go for it.' I didn't want to try it on my own say so." His brother-in-law figured the relatively small investment wouldn't be too much of a financial flier for Webb to take. But a month later super loader Doug Elik called to introduce himself and then, as Webb says, it became "serious money." Over the course of about eighteen months Elik coerced Webb into handing over a total of $34,563.25 for the purchase of several stocks. "In times past I had bought other things that didn't really go anywhere. The way Elik was promoting it was that you couldn't really lose," says Webb.

Early on in their relationship, Elik telephoned Webb regularly. With each call Elik would spin ever-growing yarns about the potential for big returns. According to OSC hearing documents, for example, between late 1992 and mid-1993 Elik told Webb that he possessed exclusive information on a company called

# GREED

Willingdon Resources Inc. During one conversation Elik told
Webb that he expected Willingdon to rise by an astounding "25
to 200 per cent in thirty to forty-five days."

In another conversation, taped in February 1993, Elik
informed Webb: "There was a little bit of a hiccup with the directors [of Willingdon] with the news that they wanted to bring forward at the particular point. It has been delayed. It has all been
straightened out at this stage and once they bring it out, as I said,
this stock will be back up without a problem.... I am telling you
right now, I can't sit down and talk to you about specifics
because I am not allowed to. There is something that is happening, you have to read between the lines, the stock is coming up.
We, as I say, are going to be crossing the block of a couple of hundred thousand shares ... when you see a block of 200,000 shares
go through, then you will know the game has begun.... I am
telling you that Willingdon is coming back in price. It is not a
matter [sic] it is going to come back in price just because I am
telling you. There are things that are bigger than me that are happening behind the scenes that will make that stock come back in
price."

However, according to Willingdon's president, John Moses,
the statements made by Elik and other Manning salesmen about
his company were either totally false or incredibly misleading.
On April 26, 1994, in a sworn affidavit filed with the OSC,
Moses said: "I have no idea what the broker is referring to when
he states 'hiccup with the directors of the company with the news
they wanted to bring out'; around February 1993, Willingdon's
Corporate Secretary quit, however, other than that there was no
news of any particular significance that Willingdon was seeking
to announce; I do not know what the broker is speaking about

when he states, '... something that is happening, you have to read between the lines, the stock is coming up ...'; I do not know what the broker is talking about when he is referring to "... things that are bigger than me that are happening behind the scenes that will make the stock come back in price.' "

Webb's tapes also revealed that on June 25, 1993, Elik, in an attempt to keep stringing his shut-in client along, called him to say that two companies, Golden Eagle and Optimal Robotics, were in a joint $40-million deal with IBM. At no time were either of these firms in a deal with IBM, but Elik promised that their stocks, a portion of which Webb owned, would jump higher and he'd see profits "by Labour Day if not sooner."

Webb attempted to sell his stocks, but his repeated requests for shares to be sold at levels that would have given him a profit went unheeded. Webb felt he'd never get his money back and thought the downward spiral wouldn't end.

By the fall of 1993, after several more unsuccessful attempts at getting hold of Elik, he reached Jill Bolton, the woman whose job at Manning was to soothe irate clients. Bolton's role was described by OSC staff as a "cooler." Usually, her seemingly charming demeanour, English accent and empty promises would be enough to placate clients, but this was one occasion where she couldn't cajole her way out. Even her offer to leave Elik a pager message didn't satisfy Webb, because he knew from experience Elik would never return the call. Webb decided to take a different tack and phoned Ted Manning, Jr., Judith's son. Like Elik, Ted Jr. was considered to be part of management and a successful loader at the firm, but after being told by Webb that his conversations with Manning staff had been taped he told Webb that he'd have his mother call him. There was no doubt that Judith

Manning enjoyed having her children by her side at the bosom of her business. Adopted son Tony was the marketing manager; Judy, the office manager; Mary Martha, more widely known as Marty, head of compliance; and Ted Jr., the consummate loader. Judith kept a special place for Doug Elik, her "supersalesman," and treated him like one of her own. In fact, Elik used to refer to Judith as "Mum." But there was also no doubt in anyone's mind at Manning, "Mum" ran the show.

Having learned that Webb had potentially incriminating tapes in his possession, Judith Manning apparently felt it prudent to give him a call.

On January 11, 1994, more than two weeks after he had spoken to Ted Jr., Webb's phone rang. It was Judith Manning on the line. After introducing herself, she said: "Mr. Webb, are you the gentleman who has told our people that you have our conversations on tape?"

D.W.: "That is right."

J.M.: "You are, so you have—is my conversation with you being taped?"

D.W.: "That is right."

J.M.: "It is. I can't deal with you if you are going to tape. I am not going to deal with somebody who is taping conversations. Let me say this to you, I am prepared to deal with you, but not on the basis of a tape recording or on the threat of the [Ontario] Securities Commission, because what you are doing is, you are using extortion to try to return money, whether you are entitled to have it back or whether you are not entitled to have it back is not the question. The question is that you are using a body, the [Ontario] Securities Commission and tape recordings to—I just can't deal with somebody on that basis."

D.W.: "You see, the reason—"

J.M.: "I am prepared to talk to you but not under those circumstances."

D.W.: "All right, let me just explain. The reason that I am taping things is because I have multiple sclerosis and I can't write."

J.M.: "We know that. We are aware that you are disabled. On August 13th, 1992, we sent you a letter, a risk letter ..."

During their conversation Judith Manning claims repeatedly to have sent Webb a letter which pointed out the risk he would assume by investing in penny stocks, but Webb can't recall receiving such a letter. He tells her that he received virtually nothing from them about what the broker-dealer did or the stocks he bought, with the exception of receiving invoices for his purchases. Judith informs Webb that a "copy" of the letter sent to him was filed away in Manning's compliance department. She also tells him that "Mrs. Fritz," the broker-dealer's compliance officer, had made sure that the letter had been sent to him at the start of his relationship with Manning. It's interesting that Judith Manning never informs Webb that "Mrs. Fritz" is her daughter.

Webb tells Judith Manning that he has since sought the advice of a financial adviser and contacted the OSC, and informs her that both the OSC staff and his adviser warned him about the perils of penny stocks.

D.W.: "... From the financial adviser I have, he told me the same thing [that the OSC did]. He has been in this line of work for twenty-five years and he said that it is very rare that you find someone who makes money [in penny stocks]."

J.M.: "That is not true. That is not true. That is a false statement. Totally false. There is a higher degree of risk when you are dealing with speculative securities. There is no doubt about that. We have never walked away from that. That is exactly what we do. We raise money for new companies, fledgling companies, companies that can't raise money any other place come to us. If we think that they have a future we try either to do a financing for them or we will recommend their stock in order that they can enlarge their shareholder base and possibly go back to the public on an offering basis, a prospectus, or raising money from the company directly. That is what our function is and that is our main business, raising money on speculative securities. We don't hide that."

It's evident that sensitivity doesn't play a major role in the boiler room. At one point, Judith Manning tells Webb that she's aware of Webb's physical disability, but is quick to point out that there's "nothing wrong with your brain."

Despite her protestations, Judith Manning eventually offered Webb a full refund on one of the two stocks he had invested in but continued to claim that her company had sent Webb a letter outlining the risks of investing in penny stocks. Then, out of the blue, she offered Webb all of his money back.

# Pennies for Their Stocks

Several weeks after his phone call with Judith Manning, Webb got a call from John Eversley, the broker-dealer's legal counsel. Describing himself as the "conscience for Manning (Limited)," Eversley told Webb that he would receive a cheque for $33,921.75. It was $641.50 less than the total amount Webb had lost in his stock purchases, but Manning claimed that Webb had actually made a profit in his very first investment through the broker-dealer, and the difference was to cover commission costs. Webb didn't quibble over the shortfall, and felt he was lucky to get most of his funds back. The cheque finally arrived in his mailbox on March 4, 1994.

The OSC's Waite, Gordon and Butler are the first to admit that the amount of time it takes to resolve securities-related cases can be lengthy; the Manning case took about two years. The work is highly specialized and very costly. But Gordon notes that regulatory and police agencies across the country are taking big steps to develop a more efficient approach in working together. In Ontario, for example, a committee with representatives from the OSC, the Investment Dealers Association, the Toronto Stock Exchange, the Royal Canadian Mounted Police, the Ontario Provincial Police, the Metropolitan Toronto Police Fraud Squad and the provincial Ministry of the Attorney General meets regularly to tackle these problems in order to streamline their investigations and see justice prevail. In addition, after having its staff cut by half in recent years, the OSC's Enforcement Branch is expected to take on another sixteen people by the end of 1998.

The delay in the Manning case was not caused by OSC staff, who were ready to go with the hearing by February 1994, but by Manning. The firm filed an appeal alleging that the entire OSC was biased against the broker-dealer, and that it would be impossible for the company and its defendants to get a fair hearing. It took eighteen months for the appeal to weave its way through the various court levels, but in the end Manning lost.

"The delay was very frustrating for us. We felt that Manning's entire strategy was to simply delay us as much as possible rather than fight this on its merits," says Gordon. "Our investigation revealed that the Know Your Client and suitability obligations, which are the paramount duties of every broker, were generally ignored at Manning in favour of fat commissions and trading profits. We believed that the interests of Manning and its salespeople were being placed before that of Manning clients. There seemed to be only one predominant question: Could the client pay for the stock? Even if he couldn't pay, in many cases the client was encouraged to borrow the money. The art of deception was often practised to successfully encourage investors to buy Manning's house stock and Doug Elik, in particular, was extremely skilful in this regard. This was intolerable and we knew we had to stop it. Manning took us to the wall on this case, and we ended up nailing them to it."

## POSTSCRIPT

Banned for life from ever working in Ontario's securities industry, Judith Manning lives in Rosedale, a posh Toronto neighbourhood, and is occasionally spotted walking her dog.

Doug Elik, also banned for life from working in the investment industry in Ontario, is believed to have moved to Florida.

Ted Manning, Jr. has gone back to using his birth name "Tim," and currently runs a Canadian Securities Course tutorial practice with former Manning "cooler" Jill Bolton. (The Canadian Securities Course is the first step towards certification as an investment broker in Canada and is considered to be one of the essential building blocks of ethical standards within the industry.) Their company, "ManTon Group," also offers a service that provides clients with an evaluation of their investment portfolio. Ironically, ManTon Group is located in the same building as the Ontario Securities Commission in downtown Toronto.

Krikor Ghanaghounian is currently working as an investment adviser at a reputable, full-service brokerage firm in Toronto.

## 5

# THE ARTFUL DODGER

Judith Manning used her penny-stock company to dupe clients, many of whom were novice investors attempting to build a better financial future. She barely knew them. To Judith, they were just a faceless bunch of easy marks from whom she and her "brokerage family" squeezed money. On the other side of the spectrum, Christopher Horne used his position as a broker at RBC Dominion Securities, the largest and one of the most prestigious investment firms in Canada, to dupe wealthy clients. Unlike Judith, he knew all of his clients' faces and their investment portfolios very well. Many thought of him as a friend and never dreamed that over time he would betray them.

*C. E. Horne, Esq., requests the pleasure of your company*
*to celebrate his 50th birthday.*
*Place: The Grange (circa 1817)*

# GREED

*Art Gallery of Ontario*
*Toronto, Ontario, Canada*
*Date: April 4th, 1992*
*Time: 7:30 for 8:00 p.m.*
*Dress: Black Tie*
*Carriages: 1:30 a.m.*
*RSVP*

*Menu: Timbale of Smoked Salmon, Consommé D'Arcy,*
*Asparagus in Phyllo, Georgian Pheasant, Salad,*
*Raspberry Bombe, Celebration Cake,*
*Fruit and Cheese, Tea or Coffee.*
*Wine: Brown Brothers 1989 White,*
*Chateau Reynella 1988 Red,*
*Cockburn's Late Bottle Vintage 1987 Port*

Four years later ...

Place: The Don Jail (circa 1862)
Toronto, Ontario, Canada
Date: March 29, 1996
Time: 5:00 p.m.
Dress: Prison-issued overalls
Carriage: RCMP cruiser

Menu: Spinach Lasagna, Canned Peaches, Tea or Coffee

Christopher Edmunston Horne was born on April 5, 1942, in
London, England. That spring had been a tumultuous time for the
British. The city and its environs had endured relentless bombing

# The Artful Dodger

by Germany's air force and there seemed to be no end in sight. Almost every night the air filled with the haunting sounds of wailing sirens as people rushed to huddle in blacked-out rooms for protection. Chris remembers his mother telling him that during one air raid she scooped him up and spirited him under the kitchen table, while they waited for the piercing whistles of shells dropping overhead to stop.

Chris spent his childhood in Bushey, Hertfordshire, a pretty town near London. The war years took their toll on his neighbourhood, but like most little boys he was intent on playing and wasn't really aware of the war that raged around him. He enjoyed peddling his tricycle in his crisply pressed shorts, handknit sweaters and polished black Oxfords. Like so many families of his generation, his mother provided the emotional warmth in the household, while his father, who was an employee of Her Majesty's Postal Service, provided the finances, but kept his emotions in check. Years later, Chris recalled that his father would sometimes ask him why anyone would pay him such a large salary as an investment adviser, intimating that Chris wasn't quite up to snuff.

Perhaps it was his desire to prove himself, stemming from his somewhat strained relationship with his father, that pushed Chris into the investment world. He seemed to have an insatiable need to be recognized as "a somebody," and he knew that the spoils of high finance—money—would help him achieve that goal. In fact, throughout his career he wasn't above paying for prestige to feed his ravenous ego. For example, he forked over $10,000 to have the foppish title Lord of Llandewy Green bestowed upon him, $5,000 to be named as a sponsor of an opera gala held in the Bahamas, and an undisclosed sum, certainly thousands of dollars, to have the Art Gallery of Ontario name a room after him. He built a career that, at its apex, would see him hobnobbing with royalty and wealthy folk, and at its nadir have him led away in handcuffs to a federal penitentiary.

Chris began his venture into finance by applying to London's Barclays Bank, viewed as one of the United Kingdom's venerable financial institutions. He was in his late teens, and although he didn't have a university degree, Chris secured a job as a bank trainee by relying on his intelligence, charm and good looks. As Chris matured he blended seamlessly among the pinstripes, bowler hats and brollies of the investment community, and was a quick study of some of his highbrow confrères and their affected accents.

Within a few years, Barclays' management believed Chris had the right stuff to climb several rungs higher, and he was offered a job in New Providence in the Bahamas. This was very much Christopher's cup of tea: money, wealthy clients and sunshine to boot. It also allowed him an opportunity to spread his wings and create a world that was all his own, where no one knew him. He made the most of it.

He spent his time in the Bahamas getting to know well-heeled, international clients who resided there. Later on he would hop planes to meet other rich clients who lived throughout the Caribbean and Latin America. He became an authority on the area's tax havens and his discreet accommodation of his clients' needs for fiscal privacy made him a most reassuring business ally. In fact, it was all of these things about Christopher Horne that ultimately gave clients implicit trust in him.

The Bahamas posting was also where his taste for the finer things of life began to blossom. Chris enjoyed attending lively parties under the Caribbean stars, and visiting clients, who were fast becoming friends, at their homes. Around formal dining-room tables and plush drawing rooms Chris would regale them with *bons mots* and humorous stories as he sipped his favourite libation, Campari and soda. Some of his new-found friends lapped up his amusing anecdotes with as much gusto as they lapped up their gin-and-tonics and magnums of bubbly. Christopher's demeanour, they thought, harkened back to a different time—the days of the Raj, perhaps—when those stationed in the "outposts" of the British Empire engaged in civilized conversation and steeped themselves in comfort.

His reputation began to gain a wider audience and he caught the eye of representatives from the international group of Wood Gundy, a Canadian-based brokerage firm, which is now called CIBC Wood Gundy. The year was 1971 and many of Canada's investment firms were just starting to develop an international profile. Chris accepted their offer to join the team. His new employers felt he could quickly establish a foothold in what they believed would be a highly lucrative business, and they were right. He moved to Toronto, assuring his many clients who planned to continue dealing with him that he would only be a few hours away by plane, and promising he would visit them often. A few years later, in 1976, Chris once again made the jump to another brokerage firm, then Dominion Securities, now RBC Dominion Securities. Today, the firm commonly known as DS is part of the Royal Bank Group of Companies, the largest financial institution in the nation.

Shortly after joining the company, he met Douglas Bradley, who was in his late twenties and a few years younger than Chris. He was fair-haired, slim and had boyish good looks. "The years have been kind to Douglas," Chris would often say. Douglas was a clerk in the company's money-market department, in an area known as the "cage." The term comes from the early days of brokerages, where steel or iron bars safeguarded the area where clients came to settle their accounts.

Twenty years ago the brokerage industry, as most other businesses at the time, didn't take too kindly to homosexuality. Money and machismo ruled. Today, some would argue that maxim has changed very little, if at all. Nonetheless, Christopher and Douglas were immediately attracted to one another and a year later were living together. It would be some time before anyone at the firm knew that Chris was gay. He rarely socialized with his colleagues and, when necessary, he deflected questions about his home life by saying that he had no time to marry since he was constantly on the road.

None of his colleagues would argue with that. The appearance of his footloose and fancy-free lifestyle—at least, to his business buddies—just added to his aura and their aggravation. One former co-worker commented rather coyly that he was fed up with "all the bull by the Horne." Another observed that Chris lived a privileged life at home and at work. While staff toiled away, he travelled the world. "It just got on a lot of people's nerves that he would prance in and out of the office and then seemed to enjoy flaunting his trips. After a while, you felt a little like Cinderella," and Chris was the only one going to the ball.

No doubt, in 1979 at the age of thirty-seven, the world was Christopher's oyster. Business was going well and he was making good money. It was around this time that he met Olga Korper, a woman who would become a very dear friend and whose influence would change his life forever.

# The Artful Dodger

A well-known art dealer, Olga believed only "serious" collectors would put their money where their mouths were. As Olga's protégé, Christopher's taste in art grew to be impeccable, but many of the works he chose were also very expensive. Chris and Douglas enjoyed feathering their nests, a mid-town Toronto apartment and a hundred-acre farm in Mono Mills, near Orangeville, with wonderful treasures they found at art galleries and carriage-trade boutiques around the world. He preferred modern art, some of which Olga described as "difficult to understand," but he also bought more traditional pieces, such as Inuit sculpture, antique silver and paintings that actually resembled what they were depicting.

In fact, Christopher's two solitudes—the art world and the investment world—played off each other in a fascinating way. His art cronies figured he made tons of money at the investment firm, which allowed him to purchase pieces few could afford. For example, on one occasion he plunked down $200,000 for a painting of a Nova Scotia landscape called *Church on the Moors* by Marsden Hartley. His willingness to pay such a high price caused quite a stir and a lot of salivating among gallery owners. Chris's homes and office were stuffed with dozens of works by such impressive Canadian artists as Paul-Émile Borduas, Yves Gaucher, Michael Snow and many other internationally renowned names. His country retreat was literally surrounded by huge three-dimensional pieces which popped out from various vantage points on the property. One was a massive and impressive eagle fashioned from railway ties and rock that was specially sent from Europe. Another was a tall, slanted stack of letters spelling "BABEL," presumably and ironically after the ancient city where, according to Scripture, a tower intended to reach heaven was built but ultimately became a scene of noise and confusion.

Meanwhile, his DS colleagues never realized that he was shelling out hundreds of thousands of dollars for some stuff they figured their kids could whip up at kindergarten, or someone handy with a blowtorch could create. Had Chris, for example, collected and flaunted vintage cars, yachts or something the folks on Bay Street could more easily put a price tag on, then one of them might have twigged to his private financing scheme a little sooner. But it would take twelve years for that to happen, and it would be one of his clients who would help catch the artful dodger.

Chris's career had continued to progress steadily within the international investment group at DS. In 1982 he was appointed vice-president, although the title at a brokerage firm tends to carry less weight than it might at a bank. As a senior employee at DS said, "Here, they make you a V.P. in lieu of a raise." Nonetheless, there was a certain cachet to Christopher's position, especially with him working on behalf of offshore clients living in exotic lands.

By the mid-'80s the four pillars of the financial industry—banks, brokerages, trust companies and insurance firms—were beginning to crumble and were about to be reformed into new, substantially larger entities. Legislation eventually cleared the way for the various financial disciplines to mix together, although it was the banks that came out on top. In 1988 Royal Bank of Canada announced it was buying 75 per cent of Dominion Securities, then and still today the largest brokerage house in Canada, with the balance being held by the broker's employees. Shortly afterwards, Royal Bank Investment Management was born, 55 per cent of which the bank owned, and 45 per cent of which DS owned. RBIM, as it is known for short, manages institutional money, as well as one of the nation's largest groups of mutual funds.

In April 1989 RBC DS's international team, including Chris, was folded into RBIM. Once again, Chris gathered up his trusting client accounts and moved them to RBIM's offices in the Royal Bank Plaza, the shimmering gold-windowed edifice at Bay and Wellington streets. Chris was happy to do so, because the bank's ownership meant that he had access to many more prospective wealthy clients through their ready-made network. During the subsequent three years that Chris was at RBIM, many observed that he cultivated relationships with the bank's employees and clients with impressive vigour.

The spring of 1989 was also when I joined RBIM and met Chris for the first time. I had been working in the brokerage arm's research department and had initially been "loaned out" to help the just-merged company with its marketing plans. I enjoyed the new challenges at RBIM and decided to move over on a full-time basis. Chris and I hit it off right away. I found his touch of irreverence, charm and quick wit appealing, and we soon became friends.

In March 1990 I was appointed vice-president in charge of institutional marketing, an area which focused my attention on corporate clients who required pension and segregated fund management. Although we didn't work directly with one another on a regular basis, Chris and I would sometimes be invited to speak to senior managers of the bank to discuss the various domestic and international services RBIM offered. I recall one business trip when we were off to do some presentations at a bank management seminar in Niagara-on-the-Lake, Ontario's wine and theatre country. We drove there in his butter-soft-leather-upholstered Mercedes on a bright, sunny day. While we chatted, Chris held steady in the passing lane all the way to our destination, despite driving at or just below the speed limit. No amount of honking from frustrated drivers who found themselves tucked behind us would budge him. It wasn't that he was doing this on purpose, he was just oblivious to other motorists wanting to pass him. This was vintage Chris—he did things his way, even if it irked people.

By early 1993 I was at home full time, having just had a baby. Chris by then had left RBIM, too, and returned to the brokerage arm. RBIM manages money on a "discretionary" basis, allowing the portfolio manager to buy and sell securities on the client's behalf without having to seek approval for each transaction. Every portfolio manager, therefore, has to meet stringent education and regulatory qualifications in addition to having their broker's licence. Managers of discretionary funds must meet at least once a year with the client to discuss their risk tolerance and financial needs. Accounts are also reviewed on a quarterly basis by another appointed portfolio manager to ensure that funds are invested according to the client's wishes. A broker, on the other hand, has an "advisory" relationship with the client and therefore must advise the customer prior to each transaction. Brokers, too, must follow strict investment guidelines as laid out by the Canadian Securities Institute, the educational body of Canada's investment industry. However, regulatory authorities decided that Chris would not be "grandfathered," or allowed to manage discretionary money simply by virtue of his experience in the industry, so he returned to DS.

In the meantime, problems were brewing behind the scenes.

# The Artful Dodger

Colin Goddard, a long-time client and principal of Valhalla Investments, would normally phone Christopher to query any anomalies that might occur on his monthly statements and quarterly reports. In fact, that's exactly what he did in early 1992 when he asked Chris to investigate something that he hadn't previously spotted: an unusual withdrawal of $25,000 made from his account in June 1991. Chris said he'd look right into it; however, it would take until August 1993, two years after the withdrawal was made, to repay the Valhalla account in full and with interest. As was his usual excuse to clients who spotted shortfalls or missed items on their statements, Chris told Goddard that "the back office" had, once again, made the mistake. The truth was that the firm's administrative capabilities were exceptionally good and "the back office" was a scapegoat he often used to explain away any problems and avoid detection.

Most of the time Chris's clients believed his excuses, but on this occasion Goddard wouldn't let it slide, so in October 1993 he responded to a routine audit inquiry sent with his monthly account statement by Deloitte & Touche, RBC Dominion's auditors. Despite his obvious reluctance to have someone check up on Chris, Goddard felt compelled to write a letter to Deloitte: "Because I have known Mr. Horne for over twenty years, I have not made an issue over this matter, but it is a serious matter, and as a long-standing customer of [RBC] Dominion Securities, I would be grateful if you would discreetly investigate this transaction and let me know if these funds were genuinely and mistakenly sent to another customer of [RBC] Dominion Securities other than an insider."

Deloitte officials brought the letter to the attention of the brokerage firm, which then, not very discreetly, went to Chris for an explanation. Chris said through a memo that a wrong account number had been used which resulted in the incorrect debit to the Valhalla account, but "the company to whom the cheque was payable was advised of the situation and promptly forwarded to us a payment ... for the credit of Valhalla's account."

But there was one glaring omission in his memo: the name of the company to which the cheque was payable. It was never mentioned. The compliance department of DS, which is the area of an investment company that ensures employees follow all regulatory requirements to the letter, didn't let the issue drop there. After further investigations it discovered that the name of the company was International Haven Services (IHS).

Christopher's memo was one of thousands he'd have tapped out on his electric typewriter during the thirty-five years he'd spent in the investment industry. He never personally used a computer for his letter and memo writing, explaining that he wasn't particularly at ease with the microchip contraptions. Colleagues at both RBIM and DS recall him spending hours behind closed doors as muffled sounds of clicking keys wafted out. Most mornings he'd be in his office by at least 7:00, about an hour before the majority of staff arrived, and would sometimes boast about the long hours he put in. He claimed he worked hard because of his devotion to clients. In a way, that was true, but it was primarily devotion to their money.

After some digging the brokerage firm's investigative staff learned that IHS had been incorporated on June 26, 1980, in Panama City, Panama. Chris had apparently approached officials at Roy West Trust to incorporate the company on his behalf, to which they agreed. They believed the company was on the up and up and that they were simply performing a legitimate request for a well-known international stockbroker from Canada. One trust official was listed as president, his wife was named a director, as was another Roy West Trust representative. Chris had paid all costs associated with the holding company's incorporation and annual registration fees, and was the sole owner of IHS.

Chris then asked the IHS "president" to open bank accounts in the name of IHS at Royal Bank branches in Toronto and Grand Cayman. As president, the man also acted as the signing officer, and Chris would periodically ask him to forward batches of signed blank cheques, which allowed Chris to withdraw funds from the IHS accounts for his personal use. In addition, Chris made arrangements for bank statements and related documents to be sent to an official with the CIBC branch in Grand Cayman where IHS accounts were also opened. Shrewdly, he never left a paper trail that might connect him to the company, that is without undergoing the monumental excavation investigators ultimately had to perform. When Chris visited clients on the island, which was fairly regularly, he would pop over to the branch to review the statements and would then destroy them. No one knew for certain, with the exception of Chris, what the accounts were used for, although they all assumed that IHS was a holding company and that Chris used it to shelter commissioned earnings.

Chris would later claim that IHS wasn't established for illegal purposes. However, evidence uncovered by DS investigators and Lindquist Avey Macdonald Baskerville, a leading forensic accounting firm in Canada hired by DS, shows that by 1982 he began to use the shell company as a means to play his very own shell game. It was then that unauthorized money from client accounts started moving through IHS in Grand Cayman back to

IHS accounts in Toronto, where Chris accessed the cash for his own use.

Throughout the next dozen years, Chris Horne befriended and betrayed a litany of people while he lived a life of wealth and privilege. Just weeks before his world came crashing down around him, Chris and Douglas were aboard the *Queen Elizabeth 2* on their way to participate in 50th anniversary D-Day celebrations in London, England and Normandy, France. It was perhaps the most exciting and overtly indulgent excursion that they would ever enjoy. The luxury liner's executive chef, for example, accommodated Christopher's craving for crackling by having the kitchen produce a roast suckling pig, which was carried out to Chris and Douglas on a silver platter. They attended a special D-Day wreath-laying and champagne reception at Canada's War Memorial in London, which was attended by the Queen Mother and other members of the Royal Family. Chris would later describe the heartfelt emotions that swept over him on June 6, the anniversary of D-Day, when a flotilla of boats, one of which carried Chris and Douglas, made their way to the same beachhead where thousands of Allied soldiers lost their lives in the Second World War. While in London they stayed at their favourite hotel, The Ritz in Piccadilly, the locale where they had for several years made a tradition of celebrating New Year's Eve with close friends. They visited Harrods and favourite shops along Savile Row. It was an extraordinary vacation, a trip of a lifetime—even for a couple who regularly travelled the world in high style.

But by the time they had returned to Canadian soil in mid-June, the brewing mess over IHS and Christopher's possible connection was about to boil over. Senior RBC Dominion Securities management soon met with Chris to ask him for an explanation.

# The Artful Dodger

At this point they weren't aware that Chris was the "silent" owner of IHS. At Christopher's plea hearing Crown counsel Jay Naster described what happened next: "In a desperate attempt to convince his superiors that he was telling the truth, Horne produced a letter dated June 24, 1994, addressed to 'The Secretary, International Haven Services,' which he had purportedly sent requesting information 'to try to quantify those of our clients who continue to have a relationship with you.' In the letter Horne refers to IHS as an organization providing 'alternative investment opportunities' and 'requests a brochure and any other information which you feel would be of interest on your organization.' " A week later, and feeling the heat from more questions, Horne sent a letter of resignation dated July 1, 1994, to his superiors.

Meanwhile, I had returned to DS to work three days a week to assist the international group with marketing materials and writing market commentary for the bank's global private client branches in the Caribbean and Latin America. I hadn't seen much of Chris in May and June because he had been away on business or on vacation for most of the time. However, weeks earlier I had invited him and Douglas to join my husband and me for dinner on Thursday, July 7. We had just bought a "new-to-us" house, as we called it, and we thought a quiet evening to catch up on things would be fun. Since I worked Monday to Wednesday I hadn't been in the office that Thursday, the day of our dinner, and also hadn't seen Chris in the office when I was there earlier in the week. Chris and Doug arrived at our doorstep a few minutes after 7:00 p.m. It was a lovely, warm summer evening. We poured drinks, chatted for a while and showed them around our house. Much of our conversation at the dinner table centred on their recent trip to England, our house and everyone's plans for the summer.

Nothing seemed out of the ordinary except when Chris mentioned that he'd have to excuse himself to visit his friend Mildred Viola Kennedy, or as he called her, "Billie." Chris had become friends with the elderly woman years before and religiously visited her most Monday nights at the seniors' home where she resided. Billie had been a secretary for a top executive at Wood Gundy, and although she was financially secure her estate of around $200,000 was modest in comparison to many of Christopher's other customers. As with a few other clients who were also friends, Chris had been given power of attorney by Billie, although this was eventually transferred away from him. Chris left for his visit and was back in just over an hour. We all said our farewells at around 11:00 p.m.

The next morning the phone rang. It was a friend from Bay Street who said he had some unbelievable news about Chris Horne. He was right. He told me that he had just learned that Chris had tendered his resignation and was under suspicion of misappropriating millions of dollars of client funds.

The news was gut-wrenching. I couldn't believe that the man whom I knew as a colleague and friend, who had been the emcee at my wedding in December 1990, would be accused of such things. I found it even more incredible that he had not mentioned a word about what was going on when—just the night before— he had been to my home for dinner. I took a few moments to gather my thoughts and then I tried calling him at his Rosehill Avenue apartment. No one was home, so I dialled his farm's number. Chris answered the phone and I told him about what I had just learned. He was very calm and cool and informed me that it was "all a misunderstanding" and said that he left the company in order to have the matter properly investigated. I asked him why he hadn't mentioned it at dinner the previous evening, and he explained that he still hadn't told Douglas about the problem. We agreed to meet for lunch the following Monday. Over the weekend I wondered why anyone would choose to leave a six-figure job behind just to have, as he suggested, something fairly innocuous investigated. After all, wouldn't it be better for him to remain to provide DS with the information it needed? Of course, at the time, only he knew the real reason why he had to make such a quick exit—so fast, in fact, that he left his cashmere coat hanging on his office door, a silver-framed photo of his beloved English cocker spaniel, Windsor, as well as art, sculpture and hand-woven rugs scattered through his office.

When I went to work on the Monday, I learned more about what Chris was alleged to have done and that the company already had substantial proof against him. It was far bigger than he had ever alluded to, which made me wonder why Chris was so seemingly relaxed about the situation when we spoke on the phone. I realized it wouldn't be prudent for me to meet with him at that point since I was an employee of DS and everything was still up in the air. I called to cancel and left a message explaining that I felt it would be better if we held off meeting for a while. Chris wasn't particularly happy when he received my message and, in turn, left a rather acerbic one for me on my voice mail. A couple of weeks later the newspapers reported that Chris had signed a statutory declaration acknowledging responsibility for shortfalls in client accounts. At this point it appeared that he hadn't admitted, at least publicly, to fraud. Meanwhile, the rumour mill was churning out stories about Chris at record speed, and the amount he was alleged to have swindled grew exponentially every day. One story that made the rounds was that he had already hightailed it out of Canada and was last seen in the Caribbean. The truth is Chris hadn't set foot out of Ontario since his quick exit from DS.

Once I learned that Chris had owned up to the shortfalls, I felt I could at least meet him to hear his side of the story. We met over lunch at the Four Seasons Hotel in Yorkville, an exclusive shopping area of Toronto, and he told me that the matter would soon be rectified, but he never admitted to fraud. He said that representatives from International Haven Services, a company he had been dealing with in the Cayman Islands, was forwarding information to DS to "resolve the matter."

As much as I had hoped to believe him, his explanation didn't ring true. It wouldn't take weeks for a reputable investment firm to provide the kind of information DS required, and his abrupt departure from the brokerage firm only prompted the thought that he was running from something.

We said our goodbyes and I walked away knowing within my heart that our friendship no longer existed. Chris and Douglas continued to send Christmas cards and notes, but I couldn't bring myself to respond. I felt such a sense of betrayal that I flinched every time I found a letter in my mailbox with Christopher's return address on the envelope. I thought that if I felt this way—having never lost money to him—imagine how his clients, many of whom were friends, must have felt.

I also discovered the sad truth about being associated with someone who has committed fraud. It's hard to put your finger on it, but you get the sense that wherever you go people expect you to hold up your right hand, put the other on the Bible and swear your innocence. You feel that you should at all times carry your bank statements in case anyone wants to review them; or provide the name of your Brownie pack leader as a personal reference. In my experience people tend to react in one of three ways: they ostracize you, sometimes subtly, such as simply averting their eyes when they see you; they're fascinated by the story and want to know more, but also wonder why you didn't pick up on the fraud; or they joke about it. Fortunately, my friends were wonderfully supportive, although one, known for his unique sense of humour, gave me a cake with a file baked in it on my birthday, which was a few weeks after Chris left the company. The occasional light-hearted moments were a relief, but, in the end, it was no laughing matter.

The media reported that in the fall of 1994 the Royal Bank had filed an action in the civil courts to petition Chris into bankruptcy. Court documents show that it was clear by then that, despite a large annual income that peaked at $700,000 in 1993, he was highly leveraged and owed large sums on farm-related mortgages and other loans. Around the same time, accounting firm Coopers & Lybrand was appointed to liquidate Christopher's assets so that creditors, who were owed in the neighbourhood of $8 million, would be repaid.

The backlash from the art world was palpable, however, when Coopers & Lybrand hired Sharon London Liss, an art expert, as its dealer to sell the "Horne collection." The works included more than seventy paintings by the likes of Henri Matisse, Betty Goodwin and David Milne, among others, and was sold through silent auction. Critics said that it would be impossible for the art to fetch prices that would reflect their true value since the collection had not been given appropriate exposure to possible buyers before it was rushed to market.

While verbal fisticuffs flew between dealers and the receivers, by spring 1996 the Royal Canadian Mounted Police were about to get their man. Corporal Brian Carlson of the force's Milton, Ontario, detachment explains that with the investment firm's and forensic accountant's "thorough review" of Christopher Horne's client accounts (their search had focused on his activities between 1987 and 1994), there was ample evidence to obtain an arrest warrant. On Friday, March 29, 1996, Cpl. Carlson and Constable Anne Doyle were at Christopher's doorstep at 6:00 a.m. to pick him up. The early-morning visit didn't come as a surprise. Chris had been informed by his lawyer, David Humphrey, that criminal charges were imminent. He was charged with twelve counts of fraud, and one of theft that involved a total of approximately $6.25 million of misappropriated funds. After spending the weekend at the Don Jail in Toronto, he was taken to Old City Hall on Tuesday, April 2, for his bail hearing.

A bail hearing, or "show cause hearing," is an interesting process. Essentially, the accused must prove that not only can he make bail, or the amount the defendant must pledge to pay the court to gain his freedom until a judgment is made at trial, but also that he won't vanish in the meantime. The accused must offer up dependable witnesses, usually people he has known for a long time, who are willing to vouch for him. The person who acts as a "surety" must be willing to promise that he would turn the accused in if the individual made a run for it. And he must also provide evidence, for example, in the form of bank statements or tax forms, to prove his ability to front the bail if the defendant is insolvent. Finally, the guarantor agrees to forfeit the posted money if the accused escapes, or does not follow bail requirements as outlined by the court.

Christopher's bail hearing, just three days before his fifty-fourth birthday on Good Friday, 1996, took place before Her Worship, Justice of the Peace, T. Jewitt. The judge granted defence counsel Humphrey's request for a publication ban, which precluded the media at the time from quoting details of the proceedings. (Christopher's trial and subsequent guilty plea lifted the ban.)

During the proceedings Chris said that as a result of declaring bankruptcy and having his finances frozen, he had "no assets" and could not personally accommodate the $100,000 bail set by the court. During cross-examination, Crown counsel Naster asked Chris if any of his "influential or affluent friends" had been contacted to see if they would be prepared to assist him in his hour of need. "Well, I had some colleagues at Dominion Securities and for obvious reasons I have not communicated with them. That was also on the advice of counsel. As far as other contacts within the community, most of them were people on boards or committees or things like that. And I did speak to several of them and they were not able, or not prepared to assist," Chris said.

Chris revealed that he initially called people within the arts community to seek employment, but was ultimately turned down for possible jobs and loans by all of them. "So, apart from the contacts that Mr. Bradley has provided on your behalf for today's proceedings you are unable to call upon any of your contacts over the last twenty years in this community to come forward," Naster said. "Mr. Bradley has spoken to some of them while I was detained at Her Majesty's pleasure, and for various reasons they have said no, they wouldn't be prepared to do it,"

# GREED

Chris responded.

It was a telling moment. From the hundreds of people Chris had known in his lifetime, many of whom were independently wealthy, and to whom $100,000 would be negligible, no one—with the exception of Douglas and two of Douglas's family members—agreed to help him.

However, the proceedings, as is sometimes the case with matters so serious, took on occasional humorous overtones. When defence counsel Humphrey queried Douglas about his understanding of his obligations as a surety, Douglas assured him that Chris would "toe the line." "And if you somehow learn that Mr. Horne was about to flee the jurisdiction what, if any, step would you take?" Humphrey asked. "9-1-1," Douglas deadpanned.

It was also Douglas's job to procure enough assets for Chris to meet bail. He offered up personal investment certificates worth $12,000 and a diamond ring which was valued at $16,900. In fact, one of Humphrey's articling students was dispatched to a jeweller's shop earlier that day in order to get an appraisal. "And in the event of a default by Mr. Horne on his bail conditions, on demand of the court, the ring is to be turned over to the court, is that correct?" Humphrey asked Douglas. "That's correct," he said, to which Her Worship replied, "I wish." In an attempt to scrape together more money, Douglas also offered four horses from their farm, Harrow's End, as collateral, but Her Worship felt it imprudent to have any equine guests residing at the courthouse until the trial.

Fortunately, the unflagging support by Douglas's sister, Terry-Lou Jessop and her fiancé, Peter Rowe, saved the day for Chris because they were able to come up with the balance of funds. They testified that they would be willing to put up their assets, such as businesses and property they owned, and stated their awareness that they would be obliged to forfeit them if Chris jumped bail. Jessop's dedication to her brother and Chris was remarkable throughout the entire episode. In fact, she was at Chris's side during all of his court appearances. Equally support-ive and pragmatic, when asked if he thought Chris might flee, Rowe said: "I think Mr. Horne's had ample opportunity to flee. If he was going to go, he'd be gone."

Investigators uncovered and added another six charges of fraud, some of which stemmed back to 1982. He was ultimately charged with eighteen counts of fraud and one of theft, all of which totalled more than $7.1 million.

The single charge of theft was as a result of Chris obtaining power-of-attorney status on behalf of an elderly man, Frank Corbett, who, when he met Chris in 1991, was deemed incapable of handling his financial affairs. The unmarried Corbett had scrimped and saved throughout his working life as a factory worker and had built a fortune, including an inheritance from a sister, worth $750,000. Chris was introduced to his prospective client through Corbett's doctor, who had contacted the Royal Bank for assistance in the matter when his patient was admitted to hospital. Court documents show that during 1993 Chris stole a total of $166,983.76 from the infirm man's account and charged him an additional $2,500 for "management fees." Frank Corbett died in October 1994, unaware that Chris was then under investigation for misappropriating client funds—some of which included his hard-earned money.

Court documents also show that Chris's repertoire of trickery was extensive, such as forging client signatures on letters of authorization, telling lies to clients about where their funds were being invested, blaming subordinates for "mistakes" that never occurred, rerouting customer statements to his home address and withholding the statements until they became obsolete, and telling his employers that he required special dispensation to obtain third-party cheques prior to obtaining authorization because many of his clients lived so far away.

Chris was once again in court to enter a plea on June 26, 1996. Dressed in a dark suit and silk tie, he stood before Mr. Justice David Watt, of the Ontario Court of Justice, General Division, as the court registrar took more than twenty minutes to read the charges. Chris appeared to take the proceedings in stride until Crown counsel Naster brought up one of Christopher's former clients, Mrs. Katherine Zeldin, whom he had known since his days at Wood Gundy.

Naster told the court that Chris had shown interest in purchasing a Florida condominium from Zeldin in May 1993. The plan was for him to give Zeldin US $225,000 for the property, and he agreed that she would be able to lease it back for her use during the winter months. However, Chris persuaded Zeldin that it would be just as easy for him to deposit the money he owed her into a trading account, and for him to invest the money on her behalf. She agreed. He actually did buy securities for her, but they were purchased on margin—where a fraction of the total amount is put down by the buyer, and the brokerage firm puts up the balance against acceptable collateral—"and created a debit balance in her account of approximately US $120,000," Naster said. Chris seemed to lose his composure and appeared to wipe away tears when the Crown counsel read aloud a written statement by Zeldin: "To think that somebody you trusted for 25 years would actually, someone who was more than a business acquaintance, someone who was really a friend who's been to see my home, who accepted my hospitality, would turn. I was absolutely devastated."

After Chris pleaded guilty to all nineteen counts, all that remained was his sentencing, which took place on August 12, 1996.

"With respect to reasons which may explain, although not justify, Horne's conduct, there is, in my submission, but one: pure unmitigated greed. Horne had an insatiable appetite for money in order to finance a lifestyle and status that he could not acquire by honest means," Crown counsel Jay Naster said, with the incisiveness of a surgeon, during joint submissions on sentencing. "In this respect, much has been made of Christopher Horne's former stature as a leading patron of the arts who spent millions acquiring an impressive collection of paintings, photographs and sculptures. Mr. Horne sat with many distinguished members of this community as a member of the board of trustees of the Art Gallery of Ontario. The Art Gallery even honoured him by naming one of their rooms 'The Christopher Horne Room.' What no one realized was that for twelve years this leading patron of the arts was an accomplished artist in his own right. Rather than using paint, clay or camera, Horne's medium of choice was deceit, falsehood and other fraudulent means. His subjects were people who trusted him and regarded him as a friend. In my submission, the only collection for which Christopher Horne deserves recognition is his collection of nineteen victims, all of whom were made unwitting patrons of Horne's special brand of art. Rather than a room at the Art Gallery of Ontario, the only reward Christopher Horne is entitled to is a room with his name or number at a federal penitentiary and to live the rest of his life with the stigma of being a criminal."

Following Christopher's lawyer's comments and a short recess, Judge Watt returned to give his verdict. Chris, who had dressed that day in more casual attire, had been chatting with Douglas's sister and warmly greeted a couple of people in attendance during the break. He looked, as one spectator observed, "like he was at a church social."

However, seconds after being sentenced to five years in a federal prison, a guard who had been standing next to him motioned to Chris and informed him that he would have to be led away in handcuffs. Appearing shaken by the notion that he would depart in such a manner, the man who had enjoyed more privileges in his life than most made a quick exit for a world where privileges are few.

Most of the things that were so precious to Christopher have gone. Much of the art has been sold, the farm and horses he loved have new owners, the Mercedes and a Land Rover, both leased, are no longer his. A full-length sable coat, which Chris bought for himself in 1994 for $30,000, is also in someone else's closet. A diamond ring that Chris had made with a massive glittering rock he told me "an aunt" left him in her will is nowhere to be found. There are, however, shreds of a life of indulgence that remain. One is a black marble grave marker, which is imbedded in the ground at the south end of Toronto's Mount Pleasant Cemetery. Chris had his title, Lord of Llandewy Green, engraved on it. Nearby sits an imposing bronze pedestal with a boulder on top, a piece that Chris commissioned sculptor John Noestheden to create.

No doubt, Christopher hadn't intended, when selecting verses from Rupert Brooke's poem "The Dead" for his tombstone, that they would be so prophetic—well before his final demise.

> *These hearts were woven of human joys and cares,*
> *Washed marvellously with sorrow, swift to mirth.*
> *The years had given them kindness. Dawn was theirs,*
> *And sunset, and the colours of the earth.*

> *These had seen movement, and heard music; known*
> *Slumber and waking; loved; gone proudly friended;*
> *Felt the quick stir of wonder; sat alone;*
> *Touched flowers and furs and cheeks. All this ended.*

## POSTSCRIPT

Chris Horne will be eligible for day parole in the fall of 1997 and by early 1998 will be granted full parole. Originally sent to Millhaven Institution near Kingston, Ontario, he was moved to a minimum-security facility, Beaver Creek Institution, near Bracebridge. Justice David Watt also ordered Chris, who is bankrupt, to pay more than $6 million in compensation, about half of which will go to RBC Dominion Securities and the Royal Bank of Canada. The balance will be divided up between insurance companies representing the broker and the bank. The money owed will be furnished by the sale of his former property and chattels. However, if these funds do not cover the amount owing, Chris will be responsible for the difference when he is released.

Although some believe Chris has hidden money in offshore accounts, a thorough investigation by forensic accountants and police hasn't uncovered any. "He has either spent them during the currency of his fraud or turned them over to the trustee in bankruptcy," Crown counsel Naster told the court.

Douglas Bradley continues to work at a secretarial services temporary agency in Toronto. He has moved out of the Rosehill Avenue apartment that he and Chris shared for more than nineteen years.

Olga Korper's Morrow Avenue properties in the west end of Toronto, which included art galleries, were seized by her largest creditor, the Toronto-Dominion Bank, in late 1996 and put up for sale.

RBC Dominion Securities reimbursed all nineteen of Chris's victims for their losses. In June 1996 the Investment Dealers Association of Canada, a self-regulatory organization of the brokerage industry, fined the firm $250,000 for failing to supervise Chris appropriately. The company paid the fine and also tightened internal controls.

Corporal Rick Edwards, of the RCMP's Commercial Crime Section in Winnipeg, donned his red serge uniform when he testified during the Winnipeg Commodity Exchange–related cases. The all-women jury at Gary Harpman's trial were riveted. RCMP

Stock promoter Eugene Sirianni in his spacious office overlooking downtown Vancouver. THE VANCOUVER SUN

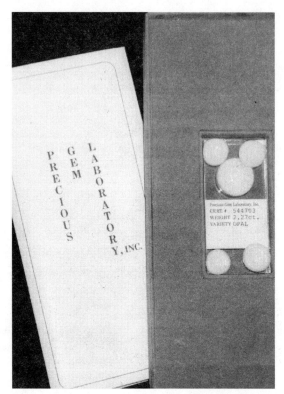

Victims of the gemstone scam received fake certificates of analysis. The stones and "strategic metals" were encased in plastic to discourage investors from checking their true value.

Doug Webb, who taped his conversations with Manning salespeople, helped Ontario Securities Commission staff shut the broker-dealer down.

E.A. Manning Ltd. was a family affair, as Judith Manning—flanked by (from left) Ted Manning, Marty Manning-Fritz, Doug Elik, and Judy and Tony Manning—wanted it. BRIAN CONDRON / THE FINANCIAL POST

Larry Waite (left), director of enforcement at the Ontario Securities Commission, and Mark Gordon, the OSC's senior legal counsel, were "on the side of the angels" in their pursuit of broker-dealer E.A. Manning Ltd.

Former broker Christopher Horne cuts the cake during his fiftieth birthday party celebration held at The Grange in the Art Gallery of Ontario.

Chris Horne loved the good life. Here, at a small dinner party in the spring of 1991, he smiles for the camera, and shows a glimmer of his charm.

This black marble grave marker features his title "Lord of Llandewy Green," for which he paid $10,000. Nearby, a boulder sits atop a bronze pedestal—a work Horne had commissioned for his final resting place.

Flashing his huge diamond ring, the fun-loving financier embraces California socialite Arlene FitzPatrick (right), with me on his other side, at the spring 1991 dinner gathering.

Christopher and I at his spectacular birthday party in April 1992. Guests received a glass cube with the party's invitation engraved on it as a keepsake.

Former Sumitomo copper trader Yasuo Hamanaka, known as "Mr. Five Per Cent" for the portion of the world's copper supply he once controlled, now faces a lengthy investigation and trial.
CANAPRESS PHOTO SERVICE

Former Osler executive Len Gaudet at the Toronto Stock Exchange Christmas party in 1987 during which a belly dancer popped out of a Santa sack just for him. No one knew that his smiles belied big troubles back at the investment firm.
THE FINANCIAL POST

Len Gaudet's former home in the west end of Toronto symbolized the kind of lifestyle he once enjoyed. PETER REDMAN / THE FINANCIAL POST

Bernard F. Bradstreet's clean-cut looks and military bearing allowed him to pass himself off as a born leader while at high-technology firm Kurzweil. He led his staff down the path to ruin. BOSTON HERALD

# —6—

# JAPAN'S FALLEN SONS

Contrary to the Christopher Hornes of this world, not everyone caught in a fraud is out for personal gain, but ego is still part of the equation. Two stories that recently captured the world's attention involve traders at Japanese companies, the Daiwa Bank and Sumitomo Corp., and illustrate an important aspect of Japanese culture—that of saving face. Unlike westerners the Japanese feel shame more acutely rather than guilt, which in part explains why the hidden trades in both cases went undetected for years. Toshihide Iguchi of Daiwa and Yasuo Hamanaka of Sumitomo felt that the only "honourable" thing to do was to hide their losses.

Toshihide Iguchi was a quiet, pleasant man who was well liked and respected by his co-workers. Despite his high-powered and energy-charged job as Daiwa Bank Ltd.'s chief of treasury-bond trading in New York, he lived a simple, almost reclusive life out-side the office. He had a comfortable—but relatively modest—house worth US $330,000 in Kinnelon, New Jersey, a prosperous bedroom community for Manhattan. The man known as "Tosh" to his colleagues was courteous with neighbours, but mostly kept to himself.

But on September 23, 1995, police arrived at Iguchi's home and led him away in handcuffs. Media reports at the time could only hint at a cover-up and possible fraud, and that somehow Iguchi was implicated. Most who knew him couldn't believe that he was capable of doing anything illegal, let alone attempt to hide a felony, and yet three days later a somewhat dishevelled and impassive Iguchi appeared in court to face almost unprece-dented criminal fraud charges. Observers feared that perhaps another Barings Bank situation, the financial institution melt-down of epic proportions that had occurred just seven months before, was about to unfold. Could it be that Daiwa, one of Japan's major commercial or "city" banks, would go under, too?

"This incident is being considered as similar to Nick Leeson of Barings, but the total loss for Barings was more than Barings' capital base," a representative from Japan's finance ministry said days after the story broke. "In the case of Daiwa the loss is only about one-seventh to one-eighth of its capital base, so this is not an issue which could shake Daiwa," he said. His bravado belied what was to come.

Wearing a sweater of many colours and weather-worn blue jeans, Iguchi remained stone-faced as a prosecutor from the U.S. Attorney-General's office told the court that Iguchi had covered up US $1.1 billion in losses from treasury-bond deals which spanned an incredible twelve-year time-frame. The charge stated that he had pilfered from Daiwa client accounts to hide the losses, and doctored trading slips and other paperwork to make it appear his bogus bond trades were valid.

(In the fast-paced world of international trading, Iguchi was actually dealing with relatively straightforward securities. In their simplest form, bonds represent a debt where the issuer of the bond promises to pay the holder a specified amount of interest for a specified period of time, and to repay the loan on its maturity. For example, dealers build up their inventory of bonds if they believe interest rates will fall because bond prices move in the opposite direction of interest rates. Basically, as interest rates rise, bond prices drop, and as interest rates decline, bond prices rise. Iguchi's problems started when he made bad bets on where he thought interest rates were headed and lost money on the prices of bonds he had on his books. Like a desperate gambler who believes the next bet will put him back in the black, Iguchi kept thinking he'd trade his way out of his losses. Even when he made a winning trade, it was never enough to clean the slate.)

The bank soon announced that it would sell 30 billion yen of its equity holdings and 34 billion yen worth of real-estate securities to ensure it would keep its head above water.

How could and why would the boyish-looking trader, then forty-four, do such a thing? After all, he didn't appear to be benefiting from it personally. There were no obvious luxuries or expensive interests he pursued. "I'm sure part of his need to hide his losses was due to the [Japanese] culture and the whole issue about saving face," says one banker from another financial institution who knew Iguchi. "He simply couldn't show that he had made such lousy moves, so it just continued. Obviously, his losses started out fairly small, and like a lot of traders who are under intense pressure to make it work he probably figured he'd get back onside. When he didn't, he just kept playing the game. I don't think the numbers clicked with him, or how big the losses had grown," he said.

But even more incredible was how he was able to get away with it over a dozen years without, it appears, anyone noticing. Ironically, Daiwa authorities only found out through the perpetrator himself, who finally cracked under the weight of the approximately *30,000 fraudulent trades* he had made between 1984 and 1995. In July, two months before he was arrested, Iguchi penned a letter marked "Personal and Confidential" to Daiwa's president, Akira Fujita, in which he confessed to the crimes he had been keeping under wraps. "My life was simply filled with guilt, fear and deception. I saw no one coming to stop me. I had to do it myself," Iguchi, who had also run the bank's securities custody department, told U.S. District Judge Michael Mukasey at his hearing on October 19. That day he pleaded guilty to six counts of misapplication of funds, false entries in bank books and records, money laundering and conspiracy.

It was an incredible journey for the man who grew up in Kobe, Japan. Iguchi also studied psychology at South Missouri State University and sold cars for two years before joining Daiwa Bank in New York in 1976. No doubt it was an innocuous start for a person whose fraudulent trades would one day turn Wall Street and the Japanese yen on their respective ears, and strain diplomatic relations between the U.S. and Japan.

It appears that, as in other fraud cases, there was one common weakness found in Daiwa's trading desks: lax internal controls. Even more incredible was the fact that the losses did not involve trading in options or derivatives, the more sophisticated and sometimes maligned investment tools that trader Nick Leeson misused to dismantle Barings. When Barings started in derivatives trading, many of the senior staff were not familiar with the high-end securities and weren't willing to show their ignorance by asking Leeson too many questions. The environment gave him an opportunity to make it appear that he really knew what he was doing. Conversely, Iguchi traded run-of-the-mill treasury bonds and bills—securities that are not terribly difficult to understand and should have been policed more easily. "I find it hard to believe that 'plain vanilla' transactions such as these were being allowed to accumulate so long. That's a real slack control system to say the least," observed Larry Duke, a senior executive at Citibank in New York.

What would be yet another shocking twist to the case was the revelation by investigators that Iguchi had suggested to the bank's top executive in his confessional letter that Daiwa should hide the losses from regulators. Incredibly, the bank went along with it in an attempt to avoid sanctions against its U.S.-based business, and presumably steer clear of a global catastrophe. Senior executives even covertly intimated to Iguchi, through some well-chosen staff, that he might be able to keep his job at Daiwa if he cooperated. Daiwa president Fujita's comments to the press seemed appropriately nonplussed following Iguchi's arrest: "He seemed very good at what he did, and I heard that he was well respected by the bond market. We valued him very highly," Fujita said.

But the jig was up when, at his plea hearing, Iguchi told the court that senior managers at Daiwa's New York office agreed to lie to the U.S. Federal Reserve Board (the Fed). He also told the court that bank executives allowed him to continue his trading activities even after they knew full well about his huge losses. Daiwa officials confirmed that they told Iguchi to sell government bonds held by the bank in New York and then use the profits to pay for the interest that would fall due on bonds Iguchi had pretended to sell but actually kept on the bond desk's trading ledger.

In an attempt to defuse Iguchi's comments, however, Daiwa issued a statement: "It is a fact that there were instructions to sell government bonds for the purpose of paying interest as an emergency step to prevent Iguchi from fleeing, but this was not to cover up."

"We were investigating trades done over eleven years. Some of the documents have already been lost and without the cooperation of Iguchi, we could not find out why this happened," a Daiwa spokesman added. "If the whole thing had become open, it would have become difficult for Iguchi to stay in New York. He might have fled, or committed suicide, which would have made it impossible for us to find out what happened," the spokesman said.

But, according to Iguchi, there was still more to the story, and to get at the whole truth investigators would have to dig deeper into Daiwa's infrastructure. Court documents show that Iguchi offered up some of his own spadework when he described how he was approached in 1988—seven years before the scam cracked open—by two other traders in his office. The traders also needed to hide their losses, which exceeded Daiwa's loss limit of US $1 million. The three, according to Iguchi, conspired to cloak the problem in unauthorized transactions.

Iguchi's claims were yet another huge embarrassment to the

company. Daiwa scrambled for cover under its statement, which noted that it was unable to confirm, at that point, its fallen employee's allegations that he was joined by others on staff to execute untruthful trades.

Meanwhile, officials from Japan's finance ministry were also about to be thrown into Daiwa's sea of red, which appeared to be rising with each passing moment. "I believe the bank can well afford to cope with this loss and that when considering their asset quality, profitability and unrealized gains on their assets, this incident will not cause any concern over Daiwa's financial strength," said Masayoshi Takemura, Japan's finance minister, seen by many as a puppet of the ministry's bureaucrats.

Although Takemura's words were just what the spin doctors ordered, they had little positive impact on the ministry's credibility. A large part of the problem was due to what had led up to the Daiwa debacle in the previous months. Earlier in the year Japan was under siege because of a ballooning trade surplus and faltering trade talks. The Nikkei, Japan's stock market, was also losing steam, sinking under the weight of a debt-heavy financial system. Then trade talks between the U.S. and Japan almost ground to a halt, which prompted Washington to flex its muscles by threatening to slap 100 per cent import tariffs on thirteen of Japan's luxury car models.

In early October, only a fortnight after Iguchi's arrest, International Monetary Fund and World Bank officials met in Washington to discuss an array of financial matters of global importance, including Daiwa's dilemma. During the conference word got out that some top guns at Japan's finance ministry had been informed about Daiwa's losses soon after company brass found out. One official was none other than the ministry's banking bureau chief, Yoshimasa Nishimura, who was made aware of the trader's letter to the bank's president well before U.S. federal regulators were informed. Apparently, Nishimura urged Daiwa's Fujita to get on with the investigation as quickly as possible, and keep him posted about any significant developments. On September 12 the bank gave the ministry another, more detailed, report on the matter, and on September 18 a formal report was presented to both U.S. and Japanese authorities. The finance ministry originally stated that it had been told of Iguchi and his scheme on the same day U.S. representatives were told. The ministry later excused the delays by saying it had grave concerns about the impact Iguchi's losses would have on an already fragile Japanese banking system.

Fed officials felt it was one thing for Daiwa Bank to discover internal problems and fraud within its four walls, but it was entirely another matter for a Group of Seven central bank to withhold crucial information from them. The ministry's foot-dragging infuriated the Fed.

Interestingly, even before this scandal came to light, there were other questionable situations in which Daiwa Bank–related companies found themselves. In February 1993, Daiwa Securities America and three other major Japanese investment firms were charged with violating securities laws. Without admitting or denying the charges, Daiwa Securities settled U.S. Securities and Exchange Commission charges and paid a US $200,000 civil penalty. Daiwa again settled charges that stemmed from the 1991 Salomon Brothers treasury-bond bidding scandal; it was charged with making a US $3.5 billion bid in a 1989 treasury-bills auction without disclosing that US $3 billion was actually being done on behalf of Salomon, and exceeded the legal limit for which one investment firm could bid. A fine was eventually paid for that infraction. On a third occasion the Fed arrived for a routine inspection of Daiwa Bank Trust, the bank's investment trust arm in New York, in 1992. The Fed was not told about significant losses within the trust firm's bond-trading operations, just as Daiwa Bank authorities would remain silent in the Iguchi case. To hide the losses, which stacked up between 1984 and 1987 and totalled US $97 million, the trust company removed bond-trading records and sent some staff to work temporarily at another branch when the Fed came calling. The convoluted orchestration of paper and people was a ruse to hide evidence that would show they failed to keep trading and record-keeping functions separate. Daiwa finally fessed up, and, in turn, the Fed notified Japan's finance ministry. The matter, which involved three senior executives at the firm, was "resolved," according to ministry officials, who also claimed to have told Daiwa to clean up their act. Evidently no one was listening.

In the end, however, the Iguchi fraud was just too massive to hide, and many people paid for it, although some not so dearly as others. Like the elaborate domino mazes the Japanese are adept at creating, Daiwa executives fell in quick succession. On October 9, 1995, Daiwa Bank's president Fujita held a press conference to say that he was stepping down to be replaced by Takashi Kaiho. Fujita didn't mention, however, that he would stay on as a paid adviser to the bank. In addition, chairman Sumio Abekawa said he would remain until the spring of 1996 to give the bank time to restructure. Fumio Kitora, president of Daiwa Bank Trust, was also slated to leave, as well as Daiwa's deputy president, Kenji Yasui, and managing director Hiroyuki Yamaji. The bank also agreed to make a clean sweep of its other international offices and, in the process, slashed about 2,600 jobs. In addition, officials said it would prohibit all Daiwa offices outside Japan from trading for their own accounts.

In early November, one month after the resignations, the U.S. Attorney-General's office came back at Daiwa Bank Ltd. and indicted the company on criminal fraud charges. The twenty-four-count indictment accused Daiwa of making false entries in its books, of wire and mail fraud, and of falsifying records. The charges also stated that the bank obstructed the examination of a financial institution. Meanwhile, the Fed decided to make an example of them. It ordered the bank to halt its business operations in the U.S. within ninety days, alleging that Daiwa "engaged in a pattern of unsafe and unsound banking practices and violations over an extended period of time that are most serious in nature." On December 27, Masahiro Tsuda, a former manager of Daiwa Bank in New York, was also indicted for conspiracy to defraud the Fed by helping to conceal Iguchi's losses. Investigators said he had failed to file a criminal referral with the Fed, postponed an internal audit that would likely have uncovered the losses, and removed records which he hid in his home.

With no other alternative, Daiwa agreed to close its U.S. operations by February 2, 1996. Although the international banking community expected that Daiwa would be penalized, the severity of the punishment surprised many. "These guys [Daiwa] are one of the fattest cats on the Street. I knew there would be sanctions, but to boot them out of the U.S. is playing hardball. It sends a strong message to other foreign banks operating in the U.S.," said one foreign banker.

After days of legal jousting with prosecutors, Daiwa pleaded guilty to eight of the original twenty-four fraud and conspiracy charges in February 1996 and paid a fine of US $340 million, a large amount but considerably less than the US $1.3 billion the U.S. Attorney-General's office originally had in mind. Ever resilient, several months later Daiwa Bank applied to Japanese tax authorities to have the fine allowed as a tax deduction so it and other losses of US $1.4 billion the company reported for its 1995 fiscal year could be used as an allowable loss. The move would reduce the after-tax bite of the fine by 40 per cent, although tax officials were tight-lipped when asked if they would give Daiwa the break.

Nevertheless, the penalty was one of the toughest ever imposed on a foreign company. However, the bank was able to offset some of its woes by selling most of its loans outstanding and U.S.-based offices to Sumitomo Bank Ltd. of Japan, one of the largest banks in the world, for US $3.37 billion. The relationship would be an unlucky one. Several months after the deal was signed, one of Sumitomo Bank's affiliates—a member of what the company describes as its *Hakusuikai* association—would itself be mired in scandal. The losses would be far greater than Daiwa's or Barings', and would give Sumitomo the dubious claim to having the largest trading losses ever incurred by a company in world history.

In October 1996 Masahiro Tsuda was sentenced to two months in prison and fined US $100,000. In December 1996 Toshihide Iguchi was sentenced to four years in prison. He was also fined US $2 million and ordered to pay US $570,000 in restitution.

Yasuo Hamanaka was looked upon as the golden boy of the copper market. Like Toshihide Iguchi at Daiwa, Hamanaka was a man who took his work seriously and was respected by his peers at Sumitomo Corp., one of the world's powerhouses of copper trading. But by comparison, Hamanaka, who worked in Tokyo, had a considerably higher international profile and was seen as a savvy copper trader in a brutally competitive industry. Dubbed a variety of nicknames, he was variously known as "Mr. Big," "The Hammer," "Mr. Copper" and "Mr. Five Per Cent," because he at one time controlled that much of the globe's copper market.

To those outside the metals industry, 5 per cent may not seem all that impressive. But by taking a look at 1996 Western consumption alone, which was estimated at 10.399 million tonnes, a clearer picture of the power Hamanaka wielded comes into focus. At US $1.20 per pound—the price of copper in May, just before Sumitomo's announcement—the market at the time was valued at around US $27.5 billion, which means, at a *minimum*, Hamanaka had control over a staggering $1.38 billion. (A tonne is a metric ton, which is equivalent to 2,204.62 pounds.)

As remote and frenetic institutional metals-trading desks around the world are, the trade in copper has deep veins in the financial well-being of global economies. Copper, for example, is essential in the production of houses and an array of modern consumer goods, such as computers, radios, televisions, telephones and cars. Not only is the metal integral to our lives today, it has also played an important role throughout the ages. In the sixteenth century Masatomo Sumitomo established the Sumitomo Corp. The Sumitomo family's immense wealth grew out of their ownership of the Besshi Copper Mine on the southern Japanese island of Shikoku. They supplied copper to Japan's rulers between the seventeenth and nineteenth centuries, as well as to the public at large. As industry grew and trade opened up with the West during the mid-1800s, Sumitomo expanded into copper rolling and steel manufacturing. From the very beginning the family held tight control over the highly centralized company. But after Japan's defeat in the Second World War, and as industry became more globalized, Sumitomo evolved into a group of affiliates, which ultimately included banking, insurance and other financial services. Nonetheless, Sumitomo Corp. remains a giant in the metals industry, which is reflected in the fact that the company's annual sales in recent years have hovered between US $140 billion and $150 billion. It also has global interests in metals, machinery, chemicals, fuels, food and textiles.

With such depth of strength to draw on, few would have ever believed that one man would be capable of shaking the House that Sumitomo built. But that's what the intense, chain-smoking copper trader was able to do.

Hamanaka had been with the company for more than two decades, the last one as the firm's assistant general manager of its non-ferrous metals division. He was considered to be an ace trader. Management thought so highly of him that he was given more decision-making leeway than any other trader on staff. Despite the admiration and respect showered on him by his superiors, investigators said that Hamanaka made his first questionable move in 1985, ten years before the scandal came to light. According to authorities, he tried to cover a transaction that went against him by using what is known as "off-the-book," or unauthorized, illegal trades. Simply put, in order to avoid showing a loss, the trader doesn't post the losing transactions on company ledgers, and in the meantime, attempts to get the deal back onside.

According to Sumitomo, Hamanaka's losses for that first

ill-fated deal were about US $60 million, or approximately 6.5 billion Japanese yen. He decided to execute more unauthorized trades in an attempt to dig himself out, but losses continued to pile back on top of him. As years passed, and as he sank lower, he found that he couldn't extricate himself from the growing hole. Hamanaka, acting on behalf of the company, borrowed heavily from investment brokers and foreign banks to cloak the losses; that compounded the problem, since the interest alone on the debt was astronomical.

Sources close to the situation said that several big U.S. banks lent Sumitomo large sums of money over recent years, and that a chunk of the money was used to help finance the tainted trades. It is also thought that a couple of the major lenders were on the hook for as much as US $500 million each, the thought of which apparently left some pinstriped executives in the banking business with sweaty palms. The loans were in the form of unusually complex derivatives contracts, some of which came due in late summer 1996. For its part, Sumitomo, known for its strong credit record, wouldn't comment on its banking situation or the outstanding loans.

Investigators from Sumitomo also ultimately revealed that Hamanaka's bigger losses occurred during the 1990s, and that he was able to avoid detection by "falsifying documents, forging signatures and destroying business records." The company said he made "extremely complex, multi-stepped transactions" and "abused his position" to finance transactions outside the company's "normal banking channels."

At the end of April 1996 copper prices started edging up after a lacklustre first quarter. In January it was priced around US $1.19 per pound. In May the metal began to pick up more altitude. Many in the market wondered if Hamanaka had been working his magic to lift the price as it broke above US $1.25 per pound in the first half of the month. Meanwhile, only Hamanaka was aware that Sumitomo was teetering on a precipice of massive losses.

"Increasingly, I think some investment and hedge funds in New York [large institutional players in the copper market] would have been aware that the fundamentals for copper were changing and they started to short sell earlier in the year," explained Patricia Mohr, senior economist and a commodities expert at Scotiabank in Toronto.

Mohr said that heavyweight investment funds saw world supply-and-demand conditions changing, partly owing to new mines in Chile and elsewhere coming onstream. The funds believed that by late 1996 and into 1997 the market would shift from a situation of deficit, where world consumption exceeds supplies, into a situation of surplus and copper's price would decline, she said. By then it was too difficult for Sumitomo to finance their positions when they had people short selling. That's why the trading losses started to really mount up.

Herbert Black, a Montreal-based scrap-metal merchant, was one copper player who came out on top of the heap. Black said he moved from a long position, meaning he owned a pile of copper, into shorting it around mid-May. The man who made his start in the scrap industry in his teens planted his bearish feet firmly in place with the belief that copper prices would move lower. Unlike Sumitomo, he walked away with his claws full of money. Some reports suggest he made more than US $50 million upon closing his 100,000-tonne position, which he accumulated over time. Black hasn't revealed exactly how much he made.

# GREED

Some in the market even attribute Black's trade as the 100,000-tonne straw that broke Sumitomo's back. For months the copper company had been able to withstand the weight of massive short-selling by hedge funds, but around the time Black placed his bet, copper prices began slipping. Hamanaka's resolve and reserves were coming to a dramatic end.

Analysts believe that the price of copper would have fallen sooner had there not been some considerable trade support of copper to prop up its price. Copper fabricators, who buy vast quantities of the metal for manufacturing purposes, had been unhappy with London Metals Exchange prices leading up to the Sumitomo scandal. They felt that the prices had been supported or underpinned at higher real levels than the open market would have dictated.

In mid-May, rumours suggesting that Hamanaka had been relieved of his duties at Sumitomo spread across trading desks like wildfire. Worldwide copper prices started to sink. By mid-June the metals giant confirmed that Hamanaka had been axed on June 5 after company executives said he admitted to making thousands of unauthorized trades. At the time, Sumitomo stated its losses were around US $1.8 billion, and feverish markets once again reacted by pummelling copper prices, which fell to a low of US 82 cents per pound.

After the initial few weeks of mayhem, demand actually picked up following the announcement by Sumitomo. "Buyers in the Far East in places like Taiwan and China felt that prices got down to bargain levels in July," Mohr says. Towards the end of July, copper had rebounded to about US 92 cents per pound, for an average of approximately US $1 per pound in 1996. However, prices were decidedly lower than the metal's 1995 peak of US

# Japan's Fallen Sons

$1.33 per pound (average for the year).

In an attempt to keep a lid on the bubbling mess during those frenzied first days, a company spokesman said he believed the losses would "fluctuate in line with world copper prices," but didn't expect them to rise much higher. *The Financial Times* of London stated in one report early on in the scandal that losses could reach as much as US $4 billion, which prompted a guarded response that it "sounds too much," from one Sumitomo official. The industry players were proved right—by September, Sumitomo announced that its losses on Hamanaka's trades had swollen to US $2.6 billion, or 44 per cent higher than it had originally figured. The huge increase was in part due to sagging copper prices, which dropped by as much as 20 per cent in the months following the debacle.

Meanwhile, observers said that, thanks to the massive purchases Hamanaka made over time, Sumitomo Corp. was awash in copper stockpiled in London Metals Exchange (LME)–recognized warehouses. For one, the LME warehouse in Long Beach, California, was apparently filled to the rafters, where about one-quarter of LME stockpiles are stored, but company officials were keeping quiet about their holdings. Over the years Hamanaka vigorously defended his hoarding by saying that rather than attempting to squeeze the market to keep copper prices artificially high, he needed the reserves in case Sumitomo's production stalled. (Sumitomo provides for a large portion of the world's copper consumption.) If expert estimates were correct at the time of Hamanaka's firing, Sumitomo apparently needed to offload about two million tonnes, or about 20 per cent of the total amount of copper used in the Western world every year. Hamanaka wasn't building reserves for a rainy day, he was waiting for a monsoon.

In addition, a report in a Japanese national newspaper, *Asahi Shimbun*, quoted the then-president of Sumitomo, Tomiichi Akiyama, saying that the company had uncovered a private diary by the ex-trader which suggested he may have conducted an astronomical US $20 billion worth of unauthorized trades every year. Kenji Miyahara has since replaced Akiyama as president. By the end of 1996 there was another report that alleged Hamanaka received "a rebate" of US $175,000 from a copper broker while at Sumitomo. Hamanaka insisted through his lawyer that he conducted all of his trades "for the company" and "not for personal benefits or out of greed."

Although the revelations about the trader were shocking, they came as no surprise to some in the metals industry who had tried to warn authorities about Hamanaka's unusual trading habits. In 1991 Paul Scully, who worked for DLT, a brokerage firm in Vermont, informed his superiors that some of Hamanaka's trades appeared to be suspect and possibly fraudulent. But in a peculiar twist of fate, a few months later Scully died in a house fire on July 4, the U.S. Independence Day holiday. Police investigators confirmed his death was an accident and that the fire was likely caused by a smouldering cigarette left on a sofa. DLT chairman David Threlkeld picked up the thread again, however, when Hamanaka apparently sent him a communiqué in October 1995 to ask him for backdated confirmations of US $425 million worth of deals. Sumitomo investigators would later say that these, too, were fake trades. Instead of responding to Hamanaka's request, a few weeks later Threlkeld contacted LME officials to have the trades checked out. The exchange, in turn, claimed that the matter was not within its jurisdiction and didn't launch an investigation.

Many believe the Sumitomo crisis will force the exchange to rethink some of its long-held and, as some critics believe, outdated practices. The LME has a history steeped in tradition and, to this day, much of the way in which it conducts business is exactly the way it was done over a century ago. For example, there are still daily, open-cry ring sessions where traders jostle for position on red benches near the LME ring and shout their bids to get the best metals prices for their clients. The self-regulated organization continues to be seen as a stodgy old boys' club where some deals are still settled with a handshake, and information is held close to the vest among a small coterie of traders. One British newspaper has taken to calling the LME "a market for consenting adults."

Unquestionably, the LME continues to wield a significant amount of power. It annually trades more than three-quarters of the world's copper supply and is a significant trader of other important metals contracts. But the Sumitomo crisis shone a bright light on the LME, and exchange officials were forced to face mounting criticism for not being aggressive enough in investigating the wayward trader. When some in the business complained that they believed Hamanaka was sitting on a stockpile of copper to squeeze the metal's price up, the LME did question him, but Hamanaka vehemently denied any wrongdoing. In a way, the LME's hands were tied because Sumitomo was not a member of the exchange and British authorities had no regulatory power over the company. However, many critics still charge that the LME's cocoon-like atmosphere and lack of transparency may have clouded the vision of its senior officials, who, they say, allowed Hamanaka to go virtually unchecked for years.

# GREED

The exchange sought information about the star trader's activities from investment firms which dealt with Sumitomo, but on those occasions the LME said it was unable to find anything concrete. By 1995, however, some cement that looked to have Hamanaka's handprints on it started to set.

The U.S. Commodity Futures Trading Commission (CFTC) began noticing extensive copper-pricing irregularities. Some people in the trade believed Hamanaka was once again manipulating the market by shelving copper by the truckload. At the same time, Patrick Thompson, president of the New York Mercantile Exchange, contacted the CFTC to discuss his concerns, which had been in part roused by industry players complaining to Mercantile about Hamanaka and unusual price gyrations. As the groundswell of complaints and questions grew, Sumitomo and the LME were pushed to dig deeper into Hamanaka's activities. They discovered that for at least a year he had been part of a trading triad known as "the Magic Circle," which included him, Global Minerals & Metals Corp. of New York and a group of Chinese metals-trading firms.

"Everyone knew Sumitomo was a big [copper] buyer; and the Chinese links would have just helped him make the argument that he needed to be doing what he was doing," said one trader. "It's kind of unanswerable, when you say you're taking on positions because you need to hedge your risks."

From the time the scandal hit worldwide trading desks like a tsunami, Japanese authorities have insisted on keeping the problem and subsequent investigation on home turf. Their unbending stance has only served to frustrate regulators and securities authorities outside Japan. Britain's Serious Fraud Office sent a delegation to Japan in late June, mere weeks after the scandal was revealed, and were told that they would have extremely limited access to pertinent information and would not be allowed to interview Hamanaka. Sumitomo claimed to have spirited the shamed trader away to "a safe house" somewhere in Japan when the investigation got under way. He was subsequently moved to a Tokyo detention centre after criminal charges were laid.

One of the most damaging accusations to come out of the case was that Sumitomo officials knew of fictitious accounts operated by Hamanaka. The company has repeatedly denied this.

Although Hamanaka has been indicted on forgery and fraud charges, there are still dozens of unanswered questions. Authorities say the investigation and Hamanaka's pending trial will likely take years to complete. One thing is sure, however: no matter what markets trade, be it copper, bonds, stocks or pork bellies, they will only function as well as the custodians overseeing them and the people who trade within them. And that boils down to a matter of honour and trust.

# POSTSCRIPT

In mid-February 1997 Hamanaka pleaded guilty to fraud and forgery, making it unlikely that others at Sumitomo will ever be implicated. By the end of February, however, Tomiichi Akiyama, Sumitomo's former president, who was appointed chairman at the end of June 1996, a couple of weeks after the story broke, resigned as chairman. He told reporters he was leaving "to put closure" to the ordeal, but said he was taking none of the blame. Most of Hamanaka's covert deals took place during Akiyama's tenure as president. Akiyama retired with full company benefits.

—— 7 ——

# TRIAD OF DECEPTION

C over-up is the central theme in the Daiwa and Sumitomo stories—both Toshihide Iguchi and Yasuo Hamanaka were masters at the game. But each was a lone
wolf who kept a secret to himself. This is a story about a pack of
wolves with something to hide.

The stock-market crash on October 19, 1987, was a harbinger of
things to come for Bay Street brokerage firm Osler Inc. Several
weeks later, on December 16, the company's three principals,
Vernard Joseph "Len" Gaudet, Patrick Anthony "Tony" Chesnutt
and Paul Marion Cohen, placed their signatures on a document
and set in motion what would be the biggest, costliest and most
time-consuming securities fraud case in Canadian history.

Gaudet, at the time Osler's chairman and chief executive
officer; Chesnutt, senior vice-president; and Cohen, president,

were convicted on November 24, 1995, of embezzling "property, money or valuable security" totalling approximately $12.1 million, of which about $9.6 million in cash made its way to their pockets. The case continues to snake along what has become an extremely long and winding road. It took the Ontario Securities Commission (OSC) almost two years, from February 1990 to October 1991, to complete its hearings and ban the men from ever working again in Ontario investment markets. Criminal charges were laid in February 1992, but another three years passed before the trial was under way. Some estimates peg the cost to investigate and prosecute the case at well over one million dollars.

Before handing down their sentences, Mr. Justice Ted Matlow of the Ontario Court, General Division, the province's highest trial court, told the men that it wasn't easy to send "a fellow human being" to jail. He was right—in more ways than one. As of January 1997 the three fraudsters had yet to serve their sentences. Even though they were found guilty, they each filed appeals *before* they were sentenced—which further extended the already painfully long case. After being handed an eight-year sentence, Gaudet spent the weekend in jail, but was out by Monday, after he put up bail of $250,000. Similarly, Chesnutt and Cohen were also released pending their appeal hearings.

"Whether or not they feel remorse is still unknown to me, but I don't think they do. It may be that their main regret is getting caught," Judge Matlow said at the sentence hearing. "The three accused are all middle-aged men of considerable intelligence ... and [they] let greed take over their good judgment," he added.

The Osler case is a prime example of how power and greed combine to make a potent elixir, and authorities say that Gaudet was the first to imbibe. He was the ringleader, but Cohen and Chesnutt were willing accomplices. Ironically, before they committed fraud, all three men enjoyed successful careers, which afforded them comfortable lifestyles. But it wasn't enough. Their cravings for riches pushed them to abuse their power, and in the end, they ruined their lives and those of many others.

Just as Judge Matlow wondered, no one really knows if these men feel any remorse for their actions. Some people who followed the trial sensed that Paul Cohen was the only one of the three accused who showed genuine regret. It's difficult to know for sure.

Research done by Dr. Paul Babiak, an industrial psychologist in upstate New York, for example, sheds light on certain people, classified as "industrial psychopaths," who *never* feel regret. Unlike "the media image of the psychopath as a person who kills without remorse, or a con man who bilks old people of their life savings," in some situations the industrial psychopath can achieve high levels of success. He says that those who fit this description and turn to fraud "tend to be void of guilt totally, and are manipulative. Whatever emotions they do show only exist at the surface. The only emotion that I might describe as true emotion is rage. They tend to blow up on occasion, but then as soon as they're done blowing up they go back to normal. It's as if it never happened."

Dr. Babiak's work also shows that when an organization undergoes "chaotic change" or upheaval, which Osler went through in the mid-'80s, inappropriate candidates can rise to positions of authority. However, both Dr. Babiak and Dr. Peter Collins, a forensic psychiatrist at the Clarke Institute in Toronto and an expert on human behaviour, caution that industrial psychopaths are an extremely rare breed and difficult to detect. Of those diagnosed as industrial psychopaths, some may be bent on committing fraud, but most fraudsters in senior executive positions are no more than greedy people who misuse their power.

Remarkably, on the day the three senior executives signed the paper indicating that Osler was teetering on the brink of financial collapse, Gaudet attended a lavish, black-tie Christmas party that evening hosted by the Toronto Stock Exchange (TSE). Gaudet's jovial mood belied the problems that loomed over him. The highlight of the night came when a Santa sack was ceremoniously delivered to his table and guests gawked and guffawed as a voluptuous belly-dancer popped out of the bag and shimmied her way around the grinning Gaudet. A few TSE and Ontario Securities Commission (OSC) regulators at the party were aware that Osler was in trouble, but Gaudet was the only person there who knew the full extent of the mess.

Unfortunately for Osler's two hundred employees, their fate was sealed the moment Gaudet, Chesnutt and Cohen acknowledged that Osler was indebted to a major client, the Canadian Co-operative Credit Society (CCCS), for around $35 million. (According to the tally of the credit society's chief executive officer, Brian Downey, Osler actually owed the CCCS slightly more than $38 million.) The firm wasn't able to make good on its losses and, in effect, the document became Osler's death certificate. Staff were told that they no longer had jobs.

By signing the document, the three men acknowledged only that they were not personally responsible for the company's debt, and that the shortfalls occurred through transactions made in Osler's fixed-income department. (Osler was essentially divided into two parts: a fixed-income division and an equities division.

# Triad of Deception

The fixed-income group traded Government of Canada, provincial and corporate bonds and treasury bills, and the equity side traded stocks.) What the document didn't reveal was that the losses were the result of a fraud orchestrated by Gaudet, Chesnutt and Cohen, and that the transactions had been executed under their duplicitous direction by a handful of mostly unwitting accomplices. Authorities ultimately proved that the three men used client money to make trades in their personal accounts and then kept the proceeds from the trades.

Don Leslie, who was then national examiner to the National Contingency Fund (now known as the Canadian Investor Protection Fund), the investment industry's self-insurance fund, testified at the trio's trial that a further $19 million was owed by Osler to its 17,000 clients who held free credit balances and/or securities in accounts. In total, Osler Inc. was under water by $57 million—losses directly linked to the investment firm's fixed-income trading department. The fund was on the hook to cover these shortfalls, which riled Canada's investment community since it would end up footing the bill. Many brokers fumed that Osler was a disaster waiting to happen, and that it was inconceivable that the senior executives had been able to use client money to blithely trade in their personal accounts for almost two years.

Adding fuel to their ire was the fact that it was not until a few years after Osler's financial problems came to light that securities regulators were even able to bring charges against the three men. In fact, the investigation and subsequent five-month trial dragged on for so long that Osler prosecutor, Crown counsel Jay Naster, was *junior* counsel when he was originally assigned to the Osler matter in 1989. In its very early stages Brian Trafford,

183

now Mr. Justice Trafford of the Ontario Court, General Division, was senior counsel. Naster, known for his intelligently crafted and eloquently delivered submissions to court, was assisted by Crown counsel Ian Smith.

While boiler-room frauds, like the gemstone case, are easy enough for the police to recognize and the courts to understand, fraud that happens within the complicated infrastructure of an investment house can be a labyrinth few can follow. Tracking the movement of money in a company whose very business is the movement of money can be a difficult task, and it's made harder when people at the top conspire to confuse the trail in order to hide what is really going on. Even highly skilled forensic accountants and Crown attorneys can be bogged down for months and years.

"You can appreciate it was a very complex matter. That complexity was compounded by the fact that we had to investigate it through a system that doesn't ordinarily deal with matters of this kind. It was a very steep learning curve for all parties associated with the investigation," Naster says from his small office at the Ontario Ministry of the Attorney General in Toronto. "How do you go about ascertaining what went on? You can't just jump in and thrash around and hope that you're going to find something. There has to be a methodology applied and one that is fiscally responsible, one that will hopefully be the most effective way of ascertaining what transpired."

After securities authorities realized Osler was no longer financially viable owing to the debt owed to the CCCS, Ernst & Young was appointed as receiver and accountants set about picking through Osler's assets to retrieve what was salvageable for sale. However, it didn't take them long to sense that this wasn't a simple matter of insolvency, and that criminal activity might have taken place at Osler. They informed police and regulatory authorities immediately.

Representatives from the RCMP, the Ontario Provincial Police (OPP), the TSE and the OSC then met to decide which police agency would conduct a criminal investigation. Detective Inspector Harold Rose of OPP Anti-Rackets based in Orillia, Ontario, who led the investigation, says the OPP was awarded the Osler case because "we were particularly interested in taking it on. We knew it would be a challenge, but we wanted to develop our expertise in this area."

The OPP then asked Don Holmes, a partner at Ernst & Young and a seasoned forensic accountant, to look into the matter. Holmes, whose deep, smoke-washed voice and "just the facts, ma'am" style make him appear more cop than accountant, began poking around. Holmes quickly tracked down a distinct scent of fraud.

"Fraud became most evident to me when we looked at the section that we called 'fictitious trades,' which were recorded in Osler's books. The client was the CCCS," says Holmes. "These trades were fictitious because the CCCS didn't authorize them and had no record of the transactions. The result of the trades was to create profit in the trading account of the three bad guys." He also dug up false journal entries which netted Gaudet, Chesnutt and Cohen a further $2.8 million, the first of which he stumbled onto was for $1 million in Gaudet's name.

But Holmes also knew that digging up all the details to prove that there was a cover-up and fraud would be a monumental task. What made it especially challenging was that a quirk in the legal system essentially forced police and securities investigators to conduct two separate investigations.

# GREED

"Our number one frustration was that the OSC had Section 11 of the Ontario Securities Act, which means that they could go in and talk to anyone who was involved. Whomever they chose to speak with had to talk to them, or that person would be violating the Securities Act [and could face criminal prosecution]....We don't have that kind of power," says Detective Staff Sergeant Jim Wilson of the OPP's Anti-Rackets Unit. Det. Wilson worked with another officer, Detective Sergeant Ed Krajcir, to investigate Osler. Under the act, the OSC has the power to compel witnesses to give statements, whereas police are not legally able to force anyone, "whether that person be a target, or simply a witness," to provide information. Police can only seek the cooperation of people they believe could help the case. "We had to be extremely careful that the information we got was not obtained under Section 11," Det. Wilson says. As a result, many of the people who had valuable information, such as former Osler staff, had to be interviewed twice; once by police, again by the OSC.

"The public looks at this case and says this duplication [of effort and costs] seems foolish," says Det. Rose. But he says the police must honour the Charter of Rights and Freedoms (Canada's law which protects an individual's rights and specifically deals with search and seizure), and that precludes them from using information gathered by regulatory authorities wielding Section 11 of the Securities Act. "You don't want to spend all this time and effort to bring people to justice and have it all disappear" because of a legal loophole. "It would have made evidence tainted and inadmissible," explains Det. Wilson. "Unfortunately, the wealth of knowledge and the undoubted expertise that the [Ontario] Securities Commission had, we had to leave aside," he says.

# Triad of Deception

It was a massive undertaking and involved collecting evidence that ultimately filled 145 banker's boxes with more than 27,000 documents, some of which went back two and three decades. "We killed a lot of trees along the way," Det. Wilson says wryly, but adds how necessary it was to gather the wide-reaching information. "Criminal proceedings necessitate proof beyond a reasonable doubt.... In the criminal context it's a higher threshold and that translates into a greater need for certainty."

Ernst & Young's Holmes agrees that it took a while before all of the investigating parties were in sync with one another, but everything eventually fell into place. "It became very helpful to me to have really knowledgeable investigating officers look at it and pick out points that they felt weren't explained well, or they didn't understand. If the investigators didn't understand it, then I knew I was going to have difficulty explaining it in court. The stronger acid test was that of the Crown. Jay [Naster] became very knowledgeable and dedicated to the detail of the case. So after that it became very much interactive with the police and the Crown and how I could make it clearer," Holmes says.

What Holmes and the police discovered was that within a few years of joining Osler, Gaudet had transformed the fixed-income department into a veritable gold mine for personal gain.

Gaudet went to Osler in the spring of 1981, and was hired to expand its institutional fixed-income department, a plan that would give the firm a bigger stake in the profitable business of corporate trading. Gaudet had already come a long way from his childhood days in Prince Edward Island, and he was keen to continue proving that his farmboy origins would never hold him back. People who worked with him knew him to be tough-minded and, at times, brusque, but that wasn't seen to be out of the ordinary

# GREED

for someone who had "made it" in the high-stakes world of Bay Street. "He liked being one of the boys ... and at the same time he could be a real prick," a former colleague says. (It's interesting to note that this is the only person who agreed to make a comment about any of the accused, and that was on condition that his name be withheld. Several people who knew Gaudet, Chesnutt and Cohen were tracked down, but *not one* wished to say anything. The only common thread from their reactions was that there appeared to be universal loathing of Gaudet.)

By May 1986 Gaudet had clawed his way to the top and was appointed Osler's chairman and chief executive officer. Gaudet wallowed in the spoils that came with the job and with his "added" income. He travelled frequently to leisure properties he owned in Collingwood, Ontario and Florida. He regularly treated guests to opulent lunches and dinners. When they weren't travelling, Gaudet and his wife, Noreen, lived in a handsome mansion in the Kingsway area, a wealthy neighbourhood west of Toronto. His penchant for living high off the hog extended to his office surroundings, where Gaudet spent a small fortune outfitting a hidden room adjacent to his office with audio- and videotape recorders, expensive furniture and a bar. It was an ideal place to hold covert meetings, which he regularly did with Chesnutt and Cohen.

Shortly after Gaudet's arrival in 1981, Tony Chesnutt joined the company. He followed in Gaudet's footsteps and was eventually made senior vice-president and managing director of the fixed-income department. In June 1985, Paul Cohen signed on and when Gaudet was named chairman, Cohen was made president and chief operating officer. They were the firm's senior managers and Osler's largest individual shareholders.

# Triad of Deception

When Gaudet first joined the firm, the fixed-income department only provided "agency" business to clients, which meant that Osler traders would buy or sell a fixed-income security on behalf of a client through another brokerage firm. Osler never owned the securities, nor did they hold any inventory of fixed-income securities. However, in 1983, things changed. Much to the delight of Gaudet, Osler's board approved the expenditure of $200,000 of the company's capital to buy fixed-income securities so that the firm could establish its own inventory. By 1985 Gaudet, Chesnutt and Cohen were the only employees authorized to trade within Osler's inventory for their personal use. That meant that they could access fixed-income securities owned by Osler, trade them and reap the rewards for their own benefit. It opened a whole new playing field for the three men—except there was one major stumbling block before the games could "officially" begin: Jim Price, Osler's chief financial officer.

Price had been with the company for several years and had a reputation for being diligent, honest and dedicated to the company. He had become increasingly worried about what was happening in the fixed-income department, and began making his concerns known to Gaudet. He told his boss that he wasn't comfortable with the fact that Gaudet, Chesnutt and Cohen could make trades within the company's inventory account and then personally benefit from the transactions. He suggested to Gaudet that it would be prudent to follow standard industry practice and appoint someone outside the fixed-income department to monitor trading activity.

Gaudet was his usual indignant self, and told Price that Cohen was monitoring the department's trading. Gaudet said that, since he, Chesnutt and Cohen were the largest shareholders of the firm, what "was good for the largest shareholders was good for the firm." Gaudet's reaction didn't reassure Price at all, and tension between the men grew. Price was shocked and outraged when Gaudet asked him to sign a shareholders' agreement, dated May 1, 1986, which sought to give Gaudet unprecedented power over other shareholders. The agreement stated that any shareholder owning more than 25 per cent of the company's shares had the ability to override any resolution of the board of directors regarding share transfers. Coincidentally, Gaudet was the only shareholder who owned more than 25 per cent of Osler's stock. The chairman informed Price that if he didn't follow orders, Price would be forced to sell the 17,000 Osler shares he owned. Price stood his ground and refused to sign the paper or sell his Osler securities.

But he knew the writing was on the wall. Price wrote Gaudet a memo, dated May 16, 1986: "You have made it very clear to me that I do not have any authority over the fixed-income department," he said. Loyal to the company, Price nonetheless outlined a number of recommendations that he felt would help improve the way things were done at Osler. However, four days after Price sent the memo, Osler held a board of directors meeting and it was clear Gaudet had no intention of following Price's suggestions. The final blow came when Gaudet announced to the directors that Paul Cohen would become chief operating officer, a title held by Price. Dejected and disgusted by Gaudet and his underhanded cohorts, Price resigned less than a month later and took a job at another investment firm.

"The departure of Price from Osler was orchestrated by Gaudet and represented the departure of the last person within the firm with sufficient authority to voice any opposition to the way in which the three accused conducted the affairs of the fixed-income department," Crown counsel Naster later told the court at the three men's trial.

Price's concerns were not only astute, but prophetic. Investigators ultimately found that one method among the several Gaudet, Chesnutt and Cohen used to defraud the firm involved the purchase and sale of securities between their personal accounts and Osler's inventory accounts at below-market prices. They would buy a security from the firm's inventory at a price substantially lower than fair market value, and immediately resell the security back to inventory at the true market price. This scam netted the three about $4 million, while Osler took the hit. The losses were then concealed by booking fictitious money-losing trades with CCCS.

Gaudet, Chesnutt and Cohen were faced with finding someone "suitable" to replace Price—someone willing and obedient. He was right under their noses.

As Osler's treasurer, Steve Wilkinson hoped to be promoted to chief financial officer upon Price's departure, but was initially turned down for the job. In fact, because of his disappointment on being passed over, Wilkinson went looking for a job and accepted one with another investment firm. He was slated to leave Osler on August 15, 1986, but in July Wilkinson was invited to meet the three senior executives in Montreal. Upon his arrival in a hotel suite on that warm summer day, Wilkinson found his bosses in a friendly and ebullient mood. He was offered a drink and after some small talk the men got down to business. Wilkinson was asked if he'd like to stay on at Osler as their chief financial officer. He was thrilled to hear that they were offering not only the job he lusted after, but a $20,000 increase in his annual salary as well. The raise would lift his income to $75,000 from $55,000. In addition, he would receive a bonus of $25,000 at the end of the year, which was a significant step up from his previous bonus of $5,000. He accepted their offer—but there was a catch.

Wilkinson was then told by his bosses that they had a problem and they hoped he would help them out. They explained that it involved a major account, CCCS, which had been posting substantial losses. They intimated that Tom Bourne, who was a trader at the credit society and dealt with Osler, could lose his job over the shortfalls. They also told him that they were hiding "Bourne's losses" to ensure the continued relationship with CCCS.

The allure of being offered the more prestigious position and substantially higher wages got the better of Wilkinson. He accepted their proposition even though he wasn't entirely sure what he was expected to do with the losses, which amounted to $1.7 million. Wilkinson was told it would be a short-term problem, of "no more than two months' duration," and that the fixed-income department would easily trade its way out of the debt.

Wilkinson was also told that he had to help camouflage the shortfalls because, as a member of the Toronto Stock Exchange, Osler was obligated to file a Joint Regulatory Financial Questionnaire (JRFQ) and Monthly Financial Reports (MFR)—documents that should accurately reveal the company's financial status. Wilkinson agreed to go along with the plan. (TSE-member firms are required to keep the exchange informed about any unusual money fluctuations and to immediately report financial deficiencies that could threaten the well-being of the company. If a brokerage firm is undercapitalized, the TSE has the authority to suspend the company's operations.)

The only other person at the firm who was aware of the cover-up and eventually participated in it was Yvonne Warren, a woman who had joined the company in 1982 and performed secretarial and accounting duties for the fixed-income department. Like Wilkinson, she was told that the losses in the CCCS account would be restored quickly. She testified that she agreed to help hide the losses because it "seemed like it was going to be for a short time."

Warren said that they hid the shortfalls through several means—overbanking (overextending credit with lenders), using fictitious "tickets" (buy-and-sell orders) and filing misleading journal entries. Clearly, without Warren's and Wilkinson's blind obedience, the three men's scheme wouldn't have worked.

At the trial Wilkinson testified that Gaudet approached him in mid-January 1987 about getting $750,000 from the company as a personal loan. Gaudet told him that he had pledged his Osler stock as collateral for some money he had borrowed from the Bank of Nova Scotia, and he now needed to repay the bank. Gaudet also told Wilkinson that if he didn't get the cash from the company, Osler would go under because he would be forced to liquidate his shares and there would not likely be any buyers of Osler stock. With assurances from Gaudet that he would repay the advance by the end of the month, Wilkinson went ahead and cut a cheque for his boss. He believed Gaudet would honour the loan in a couple of weeks, which was when Osler was required to report its capital position to the TSE, and that would be the end of the problem.

But Gaudet never repaid the loan. In fact, when Wilkinson came knocking on his door at the end of the month to retrieve the money, Gaudet informed Wilkinson that he wouldn't repay the $750,000 and demanded another $250,000. Gaudet simply told Wilkinson to "deal with it."

It was now Wilkinson's problem to figure out a way to make it look as though Osler's finances were intact. He asked Yvonne Warren to prepare a journal entry dated January 30, which debited Osler's bank account by $1 million and credited the employee advance account by $750,000 and "V.J. Gaudet's Canadian margin trading account" with $250,000. But he still had to find a way to cover the gap in the company's bank account. He had to act quickly because the company's auditors were about to pay Osler a visit for the annual review.

Wilkinson figured the most efficient way to cover the $1-million discrepancy was to tinker with treasury-bill (T-bill) sales through Osler's money-market trading desk. He then asked Warren to record that Osler had received $8,821,500 on the sale of T-bills to brokerage firm Levesque Beaubien, where, in fact, Osler actually received $9,821,500. In a few computer key-strokes, Wilkinson and Warren were able to "deal with" the million-dollar hole as Gaudet had instructed. The shortfall was put in Osler's inventory account, which was a convenient catch-all for losses.

"Any number of people could look at that entry and think it was fine," says Holmes. But even though the fraudulent transactions weren't immediately obvious, in Holmes's opinion they weren't particularly innovative, either. He found that the false entries and other bogus transactions were just buried well. "There's a myth about most frauds that they're difficult to understand. They're only made so because of the [complexity of the] markets used, or the way the transaction was done," Holmes says. "I think [Gaudet, Chesnutt and Cohen] were sensitive to attracting attention, and they were clever enough in the way they generated cash.... The major activity in Osler's fixed-income department was trading in your own account. 'Oh, we have a customer transaction, we better stop and do that,'" Holmes says, mocking the way "business" was carried out in the department.

As Holmes discovered, at times the men's deceitful tactics were convoluted; other methods were quite simple. In order to cover up fictitious trades in the CCCS accounts, for example, Yvonne Warren was told on several occasions to stop mailing monthly account statements to clients. No news for the client was good news for Gaudet, Chesnutt and Cohen.

As time went on Steve Wilkinson began to realize that he had been played for a chump, and that the "short-term" cover-up had gone on far longer than he was promised it would. He made up his mind at the beginning of 1987 that he would seek a job at another company. He told Gaudet that he couldn't "stomach" falsifying any more documents and said that the March 31 monthly financial report for the TSE would be the last one he would sign. Wilkinson received two paintings, each worth a few thousand dollars, as "thank-you" gifts upon his departure in May. But he refused an offer of a $75,000 bonus. Ironically, Wilkinson testified that he turned down the bonus because "taking $75,000 would ... I mean, it was almost criminal at the time. I knew it would look bad. I didn't want it. All I wanted to do was to get out."

The three men lost a valuable ally in Wilkinson, which forced them to rely more heavily on repurchase agreements of treasury bills with CCCS. As Crown counsel Naster told the court, it became "an essential form of overbanking" for the three accused.

It turned out that Tom Bourne, the money-market trader at

CCCS, was also very helpful. He agreed to buy T-bills from the three men at prices far higher than their true market value, then the securities were sold back to Osler's inventory at a lower price. Gaudet, Chesnutt and Cohen pocketed the difference. Rather than pricing the securities in the way it should have been done—by discounting the T-bill based on its term to maturity—the price was reached by discounting the T-bill based on the term of maturity of the repurchase agreement. In other words, if the T-bills were supposed to mature in six months (as in the day on which the Government of Canada is prepared to pay par value to the owner), but the repurchase agreement was for seven days, the T-bill would be priced as if it were maturing in seven days rather than six months. This fast-forward approach made the fraudsters a lot of money.

"Whether Tom Bourne was acting in the best interest of CCCS in committing to these agreements or was instead engaging in an imprudent course of conduct with the intent of assisting his good friends [Gaudet, Cohen and Chesnutt] in the cover-up is immaterial to an understanding of how these financing transactions served the accused's needs," Crown counsel Naster told the court at the trial.

Of the three accused, Tony Chesnutt was the only one who testified in his defence. His contention, like that of his two former colleagues through their lawyers, was that he and his colleagues weren't engaging in any fraudulent activities at Osler—quite the opposite, he argued. Chesnutt told the court that they initiated the cover-up of trading losses to *protect* Osler from going under. He claimed that they began "parking losses"—suggesting it was solely Osler's losses—in his, Gaudet's and Cohen's personal accounts because they wanted to buy time for the investment firm. Their goal, he said, was to trade their way back into the black. Chesnutt claimed that the men banded together because there were virtually no other senior officers at the company who either had an interest or were capable of understanding what was going on in the department.

"The other senior people didn't want to get involved and most of them didn't understand it," Chesnutt told the court. He added that he and his colleagues were honourable men and "policed ourselves."

Naster looked at Chesnutt's testimony another way: "Having sustained the losses, the accused were confronted with a choice: do we follow the path of honesty and honour these debts owed to the firm, or do we embark upon a path of dishonesty and engage in transactions defrauding Osler of millions of dollars? The evidence demonstrates that the accused elected to pursue the path of dishonesty."

In the end, the straw that broke Osler's back was an attempt by the trio to hide hefty trading losses of about $1 million stemming from the firm's Montreal fixed-income trading desk. On October 29, 1987, ten days after Black Monday, the day the Dow Jones Industrial Average plummeted more than 500 points, Claude Villeneuve, a trader from Osler's Montreal office, flew to Toronto and met with Gaudet, Chesnutt and Cohen. The men told Villeneuve that they had found a way to cover the losses in both his and fellow trader Raymond Roy's accounts. They informed him that they had arranged a $1-million loan for him from Lloyd's Bank, which had an office in the same building as Osler's. He was told by the men that they owned a numbered company, Ontario Limited 641893, through which they would personally provide him with the collateral in the form of T-bills for the loan at

Lloyd's. Villeneuve was given a promissory note, which he signed, indicating that he agreed to pay $1 million to their numbered company on demand or by January 22, 1988, with no interest.

It was a frantic day at Osler. By the time staff got the necessary paperwork done it was almost closing time for the bank. Villeneuve rushed to Lloyd's Bank, arriving just in time to deliver the collateral and get the cheque for $1 million. He returned to Osler's offices with money in hand, much to everyone's relief.

The problem was that the three men never owned the T-bills that had been given to the bank for collateral. They were, in fact, owned by Osler. In addition, the removal of the securities was never recorded on Osler's books. The only recorded entry was dated October 29, 1987, indicating that Villeneuve's and Roy's accounts had been cleared of their debts.

A few weeks later, on December 14, Villeneuve was again contacted by Gaudet, who claimed that Lloyd's Bank was calling the loan and demanding repayment now. Two days later, on the day that the three men signed the paper indicating Osler's massive debt, Villeneuve was phoned by Tony Chesnutt, who asked him to fly to Toronto immediately. Perhaps it was a last-ditch attempt to get money to keep Osler alive, but Gaudet, Chesnutt and Cohen were nowhere to be found when Villeneuve arrived at the Toronto office.

Villeneuve hopped a return flight to Montreal that night. Gaudet, meanwhile, was at the TSE Christmas party painting the town red—the same colour he, Chesnutt and Cohen used to paint Osler's books.

In his closing submissions to the court, Crown counsel Jay Naster's compelling words, supported by painstakingly gathered evidence, were the final nails in the coffin of the men's investment careers: "It is respectfully submitted that the guilt of the accused has been established beyond a reasonable doubt upon each of the counts in the indictment with which they are charged. The evidence demonstrates that, commencing in April 1986, and continuing to December 1987, the three accused embarked on a common design to defraud Osler Inc. for their own personal benefit. They willfully engaged in a course of conduct in total defiance of the duties of good faith and loyalty which they owed to Osler Inc. Rather than protecting, they chose to plunder the interests of Osler Inc. Rather than being accountable for their actions they created a façade made out of whole cloth to conceal their actions. They lied to the regulator. They lied to their fellow officers, directors and shareholders. They even lied to their friends. Their gains were the firm's losses. Their successes the firm's failures. Their riches the firm's impoverishment. They chose to conduct their affairs in a manner which any reasonable decent person would consider dishonest and unscrupulous. The evidence respecting each of the counts in the indictment demonstrates this beyond a reasonable doubt."

Gaudet's, Chestnutt's and Cohen's greed had killed Osler in January 1988 and after more than eight years the Osler saga had finally drawn to a close.

Naster says he is the first to acknowledge that the likes of an Osler case, with the time and money it took to investigate, should never be repeated. However, the Crown counsel believes that there are many lessons to be learned from the case and, as a result, changes have been made for the better.

In recent years, the process by which police agencies and securities regulators in Ontario deal with suspected criminal

# GREED

fraud cases has dramatically altered. Partly as a result of the Osler case, and mostly because of budget constraints and personnel cutbacks, authorities unveiled in June 1996 the Securities Enforcement Review Committee (SERC), made up of representatives from the RCMP, the OPP, the Metropolitan Toronto Police Fraud Squad, the TSE, the OSC, the Investment Dealers Association (IDA) and the Ministry of the Attorney General. Spearheaded by Crown attorney Naster, SERC meets regularly to decide on the most efficient way in which to handle securities-related cases. The committee's goal is to bring together the brain power and resources of each group, while ensuring that no group works at cross purposes.

Looking back, Naster says: "I often think about what goes on in [fraudsters'] minds. What are they thinking? How do they take into account the potential downside of their conduct? I don't know the answer to that. It's the $64,000 question, particularly where you see certain conduct engaged in which really admits to no defence."

## POSTSCRIPT

Gaudet, Chesnutt and Cohen are awaiting appeal hearings and continue to fulfil their bail requirements by regularly reporting in with police. Banned for life from the investment industry, they've taken jobs outside the brokerage community to make a living. They have not been allowed to leave the province of Ontario since their convictions.

Tom Bourne, former money-market trader at the Canadian Co-operative Credit Society, now resides in Florida. He was never criminally charged.

## —8—

# AN OFFICER
# AND A FRAUDSTER

Executives at the very top of a corporation are generally rewarded with fat paycheques, and sometimes they also receive "perks," such as big bonuses, generous expense accounts, company cars—the list goes on. However, as in the Osler case, there are those top executives who feel that they haven't been "rewarded" with what they believe they deserve— so they go ahead and illegally take what they want. In the aftermath of downsizing and cutbacks companies are expecting a lot more from their senior managers these days, so if executives want more lolly, they are first expected to deliver the goods in a big way. Former high-technology executive Bernard F. Bradstreet certainly delivered the goods, but it was to warehouses so that he could hide equipment and make sales revenues look as though they were in far better shape than they actually were.

# GREED

Bernard Bradstreet was an officer and a gentleman. Many still believe he is a gentleman, but to others Bradstreet is nothing more than a convicted fraudster.

Bradstreet, the former chief executive officer of high-technology company Kurzweil Applied Intelligence Inc. of Waltham, Massachusetts, was found guilty in May 1996 of masterminding a wide-reaching cover-up that began four years previously at the company. The scheme involved hiding and shredding important corporate documents, erroneously reporting sales on product that hadn't actually been sold, and sending the unsold goods to a warehouse to make it appear as though the items had been delivered to customers. Prosecutors also proved that Bradstreet influenced and elicited help from several employees, some as high-ranking as vice-president for sales Thomas Campbell, and Kurzweil's treasurer, Debra Murray, to carry out the plan.

But Bradstreet, who is in his fifties, is an enigma. He doesn't seem to fit the "common characteristics" of a fraudster, such as being "greedy," "glib" or "boastful." He is articulate, and as one who worked with Bradstreet described him, "he was a straight shooter." He is also very well educated. Bradstreet took his undergraduate degree at Harvard, the prestigious Ivy League college in Cambridge, Massachusetts, and he later obtained another degree from Harvard's Business School. He is well known for his devotion to his wife, Carol, and is a proud and loving father of their three children. He is the kind of man a neighbour once described as a "pillar of the community" and as someone always willing to help out when there was a need.

By all outward appearances Bradstreet was also financially secure. He made US $200,000 a year and lived on a beautiful five-acre spread in the wealthy suburb of Sudbury, Massachusetts. All three of his children attended private schools. However, records show that his finances weren't as healthy as some around him presumed. In the early '80s he held a mortgage of about US $220,000, but within a decade it had grown to just under US $450,000. He had debt, but no more than many of his neighbours or colleagues. What he stood to gain as a result of the cover-up he orchestrated at the company wasn't a huge amount, either. Bradstreet only owned a little more than 3 per cent of his company's shares, which meant that had he sold all of his holdings when Kurzweil's stock went public in 1993, he would have made almost US $1 million. At the time, he chose to sell only about US $150,000 worth of his stock which, in the social and corporate worlds he travelled in, would be considered a small amount of cash. People who knew Bradstreet say that he never would have jeopardized all the things that he held so dear—his family, a pristine reputation and a solid career record—just for money. There seems to be some truth to that.

There's no doubt, however, that Bradstreet knew the value of a buck. He worked very hard for his money, some feel a little too hard. He seemed to have a deep need to succeed and secure a strong financial future for himself and his family. Part of that desire likely stems from his time at college and in the military, places where he was taught to reach for the top. Following high school, he obtained his Harvard education through a Naval Reserve Officer Training Corps (NROTC) scholarship, unlike his mostly wealthy schoolmates whose parents paid their tuition fees. By enrolling in the NROTC program he committed to joining the armed forces for four years following his undergraduate schooling. After he received his first degree in 1967, he joined the Marines and trained as a tactical jet pilot. He went overseas from 1970 to 1971 and was stationed in Japan. He spent much of his time on combat air patrol throughout the Far East, including forays over Korea.

Bradstreet ultimately became an air-combat tactics instructor and stayed in the corps for five and a half years, eighteen months longer than he was obliged to do. It reveals something about his personality. Bradstreet lived by the maxim that if there was a job to do, you did it well and you always put in extra effort.

The Marines suited Bradstreet to a tee. He admired the corps' sense of discipline and decorum. In fact, following his honourable discharge from active duty in the early '70s, he continued to sport close-cropped hair and favoured conservative but impeccably tailored suits when he was an executive at Kurzweil and other firms. Both his superiors and subordinates knew him as a disciplined and intelligent leader and gifted pilot. They could always count on Captain Bradstreet, or "Brad," as some would call him, to keep his cool if he found himself in a tight spot. It was a characteristic that he would call upon years later in his business life. Bradstreet also liked the fact that the Marines only accepted the best of the best, that they included in their ranks some of the most highly trained soldiers in all of the U.S. armed forces. There is no question that Bradstreet had the right stuff. He was the embodiment of the Marine credo: *Semper Fidelis— Always Faithful.* As another former Marine says, "we are taught to set the example."

Bradstreet ultimately didn't set much of an example to his employees, friends or family, but as Stuart Douglas, a forensic accountant and partner at Deloitte & Touche in Toronto, explains, men like Bradstreet get so wrapped up in their goals that they "lose their sense of direction." Often they develop a "distorted kind of loyalty" for the company and end up rational-izing their actions because, in order to get results, "they'll do what they believe is necessary because they don't want to look like failures," says Douglas.

Following his military stint he returned to Harvard to obtain a master's degree in business administration. Upon graduation Bradstreet took a job as a loans officer based in Boston with the First National Bank of Chicago. From there he became treasurer at a computer company where he further developed his abilities in the high-technology field. People were impressed with his many talents and those skills were noticed by Mike Tomasic, then president of Kurzweil Inc.

Tomasic offered Bradstreet an exciting opportunity by inviting him to join the firm as vice-president and chief financial officer. Bradstreet felt that the company had "a huge potential market yet no established competition" at the time, so he decided to make the jump in June 1985 and take on Kurzweil's challenges.

The company was like a lot of firms that have brilliant ideas but not enough capital. It had been struggling to launch an inno-vative technology that was the brainchild of the company's founder, Ray Kurzweil. Considered a high-tech wunderkind, Kurzweil had already invented a machine that could scan printed material and read it aloud through synthesized speech by the time he was in his twenties. The machine provided the blind with a useful alternative to Braille. He started his company in 1982 after developing another prototype of speech-recognition tech-nology. This technology allowed the user, with the help of a com-puter and software, to translate the spoken word into typed form without the need to peck it out on a keyboard.

"Ray Kurzweil was a pioneer in speech-recognition

technology. If anything, he was a decade too early until reasonably priced desktop computers had the high-processing speed required to take advantage of his brilliance and to fully utilize the genius of his designs," says a high-technology portfolio manager who followed Kurzweil's work for more than fifteen years.

When Bradstreet joined the firm, Kurzweil's creation had a 1,000-word capacity, but it still wasn't commercially viable. Kurzweil knew that if it could be expanded it could be used for many different applications. In order to move into the bigger leagues, the company had to create a large-vocabulary product.

Kurzweil Inc. continued limping along a while longer, and in the fall of 1987 Tomasic left the company. Bradstreet was asked to fill in as president on an interim basis, but while the search was on to fill the top spot, company directors noticed his take-charge manner and began showing interest in his bold plans. Bradstreet suggested an approach to take Kurzweil from its minor-league status to what he believed would be a hugely successful operation. His strategy involved scrapping the old product, leaving the long-held hardware side of the business entirely, and focusing exclusively on developing new and improved software. Bradstreet felt that the medical industry, for example, would be an ideal area to market their product. He reasoned that doctors, who have notoriously poor handwriting, would find it immensely helpful and a valuable time-saver if they could simply "speak" their notes into a system and have them transformed into writing. He explained to the board that they and Kurzweil's investors would have to be patient and have implicit faith in the company's ability to create such a product. He said it would likely take twelve to eighteen months before a marketable technology was ready. The board was impressed and agreed with

# An Officer and a Fraudster

Bradsteet's plan, and showed their faith in him by appointing him president and chief operating officer.

In March 1989 the company introduced its first large-vocabulary speech-recognition system, which the firm believed would enable it to carve out a much bigger slice of the market. But many of Kurzweil's sales staff were laid off during the product's development stage and the company chose not to rehire them when the new technology was ready to sell. Company brass wanted to make a fresh start with their new product's launch, so Kurzweil hired Thomas E. Campbell, a sales and marketing expert, as vice-president in charge of sales and service to lead the charge. Like Bradstreet, Campbell believed the technology would sell well.

But both men knew they were under the gun, and with each passing day they would have to provide solid sales numbers to satisfy both the board of directors and potential investors. The pressure was on. It also presented them with a kind of chicken-and-egg problem because Bradstreet felt it was equally important to "take the company public," or offer the public shares in the firm through the stock market. Kurzweil had made other attempts between 1989 and early 1992 at raising funds privately, which attracted some investors. But to raise any significant money to help develop their technology and expand operations they had to go public, and to do that, they needed strong sales.

This was around the time when procedures at Kurzweil started to fall by the wayside. Bradstreet and Campbell decided to loosen the rules, at first just a little, to give sales staff extra time to sign on customers. Some even think that the men's actions at this point were justified—that they were simply trying to achieve the numbers that everyone had been expecting.

# GREED

It seems, however, that Bradstreet was willing to do just about anything to ensure Kurzweil Inc.'s success. He was very proud of the firm. "This was a company that had the potential to be a very large, very profitable, public company with both access to capital in the public markets and the liquidity of the public markets," Bradstreet explained about the need for Kurzweil to raise funds from outside investors.

The initial public offering, or IPO, is a key step in the growth of a young company. It's really where the firm gets to test its wings in a public arena. The IPO involves many things, including setting the company's price per share at which it will be offered, and creating a prospectus so that potential investors get a sense of what the company is all about. The prospectus is an important document that gives a "full, true and plain disclosure of all material facts relating to the securities offered," as the investment industry requires.

But Debra Murray, former treasurer at Kurzweil, eventually told authorities that Bradstreet was bent on taking the company public and it was his all-consuming desire that forced them into a cover-up. "Mr. Bradstreet had a discussion with me about how it would be very difficult to do another private placement round. We would be giving away too much of the company at that time [by selling another chunk of the firm to private investors]. We really needed to bring the company public," she said.

Murray, a soft-spoken woman who had worked with Bradstreet for several years, dutifully obeyed her boss's orders—even when he requested that non-existent sales should be booked as actual sales. Although she only had a diploma from a secretarial school, Murray was no slouch. She had passed all of the written tests to become an accountant, and had steadily moved up the ranks at Kurzweil because of her skills with numbers. There is no doubt that she realized that Bradstreet's demands were, at first, somewhat questionable, and as time passed, illegal. But it was the "significant pressure" to "get revenues as high as possible" that clouded the judgment of many at Kurzweil, including herself, Murray said. Apparently, Bradstreet believed that the only way Kurzweil could go public was to post six consecutively healthy quarters, or eighteen straight months of good business.

In fact, business was looking up by the first quarter of 1992. Kurzweil Inc. had just reported a small profit of US $111,000 on revenues of US $10.5 million in 1991. The challenge for Bradstreet and his staff was to keep that ball rolling and see to it that sales began climbing. The other challenge for Kurzweil sales staff was to persuade hospitals and medical centres to change over to an entirely new medical record system that came with a big price tag. The process would take a lot of time, which Kurzweil staff didn't have an abundance of, so Bradstreet cut them some slack. He began allowing sales to be put on Kurzweil's books early—before deals were actually signed.

Early on, if staff were close to a deal as a quarter was about to close, then they'd get a few extra days to make the sale. No auditor would be any the wiser, Bradstreet reasoned, because the sale would soon be officially completed. But sales in 1992 weren't going as well as everyone had hoped, and so the time between posting the sale in the company ledgers and actually bagging the sale began to stretch. First it was a few days, then it grew to two weeks. By 1993 "there was no time period," Murray said, and staff were allowed whatever time they needed to make the sale. In the meantime, "unsold" goods were shipped to a local warehouse, FOB America in Chelsea, Massachusetts, then sent to customers when the deal was legitimately signed.

Shipping goods to warehouses on an interim basis isn't illegal, nor is it all that uncommon. It simply provides a place for the equipment to be held "temporarily," then it's sent to the customer when the paperwork is complete and they're ready to receive it. But under generally accepted accounting principles, a sale can only be counted when goods leave the company's premises en route to the customer.

Kurzweil staff weren't just creative with the way in which they used time, they also became "creative writers" as some turned to forging customer signatures to make it appear that a sale had been authorized. The first occasion, it appears, came at the end of 1992 when Tom Campbell realized that his staff wouldn't meet sales quotas. James Hasbrouck, a salesman from their Atlanta office, eventually told authorities that Campbell had been putting heavy pressure on him to complete the sales orders from a couple of Georgia-based hospitals. Although he told his boss that the clients weren't even close to signing, Hasbrouck said he finally succumbed to Campbell's demand and forged both customers' names on sales documents.

Treasurer Murray said that Campbell later talked to her about the bogus orders and even confided to her that the clients' signatures were forgeries. She said that she "was surprised but I just told [Campbell] okay." She then went to Bradstreet and told him "that rumour had it that Jim Hasbrouck had signed the paperwork, not the customers," and asked him what to do about it. Murray said that Bradstreet told her not to worry because plans were in the works to change the company's fiscal year end to January 31 from its original December 31 date, and that would allow them an extra month to "fix the problem," or close the deal.

However, Hasbrouck never did win the business and when the January 31 year-end deadline came and went, Murray continued to seek Bradstreet's advice about what to do with the fake orders. Murray said that Bradstreet eventually told her to keep the bogus orders on the books which, had they been real, would have been worth US $221,000 to Kurzweil Inc. Bradstreet told her that the company "needed to meet [a] certain revenue number in order for the public offering to continue." In the meantime, the equipment for this order and others like it continued gathering dust at the warehouse.

On other occasions Campbell and his sales staff were actually able to get clients to sign sales quotes by telling them that the paper just committed Kurzweil to a price and didn't bind the client to the deal. In fact, they would use "quotes" as documentation for actual sales.

The covert plan came close to being exposed when Coopers & Lybrand, Kurzweil's accountants, who were conducting an annual audit review, sent letters to customers—including the clients Hasbrouck claimed to have signed contracts with—asking for confirmation of their orders. After several heart-pounding days, Hasbrouck was able to secure an unsigned confirmation letter from one of the clients. He forged the customer's name on it and faxed it to Coopers & Lybrand, who, based on false documents, were led to believe that all was well at Kurzweil.

Sales continued to be lacklustre as the company approached the summer of 1993, the time when they had planned to launch their share offering. There were some tense moments for everyone involved in the cover-up, because they knew that this was a particularly important period for sales to "look" good. Murray said that Bradstreet again allowed her to document sales that had not been legitimately completed. It was also around this point that Bradstreet directly tied himself to the scheme, which would later help authorities prove his involvement. He signed and faxed a "side letter," a document that only acknowledges a potential sale between the buyer and seller, to the client that indicated a US $450,000 order was in the works. But he then ordered Murray to book it as a done deal.

With several "much improved" sales quarters under its belt, said Murray, Kurzweil Inc. was able to pull off its public stock offering on August 24, 1993, without a hitch—at least not anything that was obvious to the public, auditors or the stock offering's underwriters. Kurzweil's share price left the starting gate at US $10 a share and 2.4 million of them were scooped up by investors. It was a much needed injection of US $24 million into Kurzweil's coffers.

Bradstreet continued playing the role as fearless leader and with the stock offering now complete, he felt that business could truly make a turnaround. That didn't quite happen. In fact, nothing panned out the way he had hoped.

The next hurdle was yet another audit scheduled for early 1994 and Murray was worried about the pending review. She decided to ask some underlings to destroy certain files because she knew that if the auditors found them, their scheme would be exposed. She also talked to Bradstreet about the need to document a substantial sale to fool Coopers & Lybrand into thinking that business was going well. She said that Bradstreet told her to get paperwork ready that showed that Florida Health Care Inc. had agreed to buy equipment from Kurzweil. She was then to take the forms to Tom Campbell, which she did. The next day the "signed" papers were sitting in her in-box on her desk with what allegedly was David Spearin's signature on them. Spearin, who at the time worked as a marketing representative for Florida Health, later told authorities that it was not his signature and that he never agreed to purchase the goods, worth US $274,000, on behalf of his company. "We never even came close to buying this equipment," he said.

Murray also said that the signature appeared to be Campbell's writing. Campbell had to sign papers a second time when the auditors chose to ask Florida Health for a confirmation letter of the deal—and once again his forgery worked.

But another little piece of paper caught the eye of a Coopers & Lybrand accountant who was doing a routine check of shipping invoices. The document showed a charge for nine months' storage to Kurzweil Inc. on an order that was supposed to have been shipped to the client the previous year. The auditors called Kurzweil Inc. to find out what the charge meant. Murray and Bradstreet responded by saying it was probably a simple mistake, but their feeble explanation didn't satisfy the accountants. Coopers & Lybrand thought it would be best to follow up with a thorough look at everything Kurzweil had in storage at FOB America, the "temporary" holding pen where equipment stayed prior to delivery to clients.

But in a move akin to what The Three Stooges might dream up, Murray and Bradstreet scrambled to have twenty-one skids of computer equipment shipped from FOB America to a warehouse on Cape Cod so that they could hide it from the auditors.

Incredibly, even after Kurzweil's outside directors hired the legal firm of Hale & Dorr of Boston to investigate, and with the lawyers and Coopers & Lybrand accountants crawling all over the place, Bradstreet kept his cool. Murray later said that her boss was still planning to make it look as though customers were sending goods back to Kurzweil. He gave instructions to employees to have the equipment sitting in the Cape Cod warehouse sent to another warehouse on Rhode Island because they needed return authorizations to make it appear as though customers no longer wanted the goods.

Unfortunately for Bradstreet, Murray, unlike her boss, didn't have the steely reserve of a Marine. On May 17, 1994, about a month after the storage invoice was first noticed by the auditors, she confided to a Hale & Dorr lawyer that there had been an elaborate scheme going on for some time. She confessed that not only was she involved, but that it included many people from the company—from junior staff all the way to the very top of the corporation. She said that it began innocently enough, as a means to give sales staff some leeway, but then Bradstreet eventually took over the controls and piloted the plan into a huge cover-up and fraud. Murray divulged everything, and even described how one junior accounting clerk fooled auditors by creatively using three different inks for sales entries on Kurzweil's ledgers.

Soon after Murray's revelations, she, Bradstreet, Campbell and other executives were forced to leave Kurzweil. The entire accounting staff at Kurzweil and most of the sales staff were also let go. Police eventually laid conspiracy and fraud charges against the three senior executives, but by cooperating with police Debra Murray, who faced a maximum of five years in prison, was ultimately granted parole. Authorities didn't lay criminal charges against several former sales people at Kurzweil who forged documents, because prosecutors needed them to testify against Bradstreet and Campbell.

However, at Bradstreet's trial in the spring of 1996 he told the court a story quite different from what Murray and other staff recalled. He testified that it was Murray who orchestrated the cover-up and that she was "absolutely panicked" when auditors appeared to be closing in on the scam. He also claimed that he had no prior knowledge about the unusual method of counting sales and had nothing to do with the plan. Bradstreet also said that he only found out about the surreptitiously moved equipment when Murray told him about it, and that he was planning to "solve the problem" by providing "an accurate report of the transactions." All he was attempting to do was the "right thing," he said.

But the jury didn't buy his explanations. They found it impossible to believe that someone as "disciplined" and "honourable" as Bernard Bradstreet would fail to immediately report what he said were Debra Murray's illegal actions to the board of directors, or the auditors. They also couldn't quite see someone with his leadership qualities and incisive mind not knowing what was going on at his company.

Two weeks before Christmas 1996 both Bradstreet and Campbell were sentenced. The former Marine stood at attention before U.S. District Judge Richard G. Stearns as he was sentenced to two years and nine months and ordered to pay a fine of US $2.3 million. His first full day of incarceration was Friday, December 13, a day Bradstreet will no doubt remember as unlucky. However, many observers believe he was fortunate to be given such a light sentence, since he could have served up to ten years in prison. Campbell, who could have received nearly six years, was sentenced to eighteen months. Those familiar with the case say the sentences were lenient because of Bradstreet's and Campbell's previously lily-white records.

# GREED

First Assistant U.S. Attorney Mark Pearlstein said the sentences, nonetheless, sent a clear message that the U.S. government was taking aim at white-collar criminals. "This type of criminal conduct will no longer be tolerated," he said.

## POSTSCRIPT

When news of the scandal first hit markets, the company's stock price went into freefall and hovered around a couple of dollars per share from its lofty highs of US $20.50 per share in late 1993. It still hadn't fully recovered by the time the two men were sentenced, and continued wafting around US $3.50 per share at the end of 1996.

In the aftermath of the fraud and subsequent purge of senior staff, Ray Kurzweil, now chief technical officer, is the only top manager who remains at the firm. "Crisis specialist" Thomas E. Brew, Jr., who was parachuted into Kurzweil Inc. and replaced Bradstreet as CEO, continues to rebuild the company.

# CONCLUSION

There is no sphere of human thought in which it is easier
to show superficial cleverness and the appearance of superior wisdom than in discussing questions of currency and
exchange.

*Winston Churchill*
*House of Commons, September 28, 1949*

As the world prepares for a new millennium, many
people wonder how many more Barings, Daiwa or
Sumitomo scandals are lurking around the corner. The
rapid evolution of technology has made that question and others
like it a challenge to answer: How many more millions, even billions, will be bilked from innocent people? Which of the penny
stocks floating around cyberspace are legitimate? What is and

isn't real in the marketplace? Will the sophistication of global markets make it almost impossible to detect slick rogue traders?

The Reverend Dr. Frank Brisbin, a member of the Canadian Centre for Ethics & Corporate Policy and minister emeritus of the Metropolitan United Church in Toronto, wonders about these questions, too. The headline-grabbing debacles are deeply worrying, he says, but he thinks they are overshadowing even more fundamental issues. Dr. Brisbin believes one problem is that the "Almighty Buck" has supplanted the Almighty, or, at least, basic values. That's not to say that Dr. Brisbin feels that anyone who puts money in the capital markets is bad—he, too, invests in stocks and bonds. It's a matter of rediscovering values and getting people to live more effectively by them, he says, instead of striving to turn every waking minute into a quest for making money.

But Dr. Brisbin says that to get back to the basics, especially in the workforce, both workers and company brass have to begin showing mutual respect and higher moral standards. "Fairness and morality" in the corporate world have to be embodied by everyone—"from clerks to chief executive officers," he says.

He also believes that technology shouldn't be made the scapegoat for crimes of morality, like fraud. Dr. Brisbin, who is in his seventies, is a fan of technology. He regularly e-mails his grandchildren in Australia and across Canada and surfs the Net. "It goes back to the people using it," he says. "Used appropriately, technology is a wonderful thing," he says.

Unfortunately, there are plenty who don't use it the right way, as Inspector Earl Moulton of the Royal Canadian Mounted Police in Vancouver can confirm. Moulton, who heads up the force's West Coast–based Commercial Crime Section, sees first-hand how technology easily gets bent out of shape in the wrong hands. The fraudsters he tracks down do it every day.

Criminals are "using technological means in a much more effective manner to do the same old crimes in new ways. Some of them use hacking methods to get into bank mainframes or a company's databank. Others set up boiler-room operations on the Internet to flog penny stocks on the Vancouver Stock Exchange [and other exchanges]. There are endless ways to use technology fraudulently," says Moulton. Another problem is that the "upload of information and the control over where it goes creates major jurisdictional problems that haven't been resolved yet," he says.

Moulton admits to being somewhat "cynical. At one time I thought [the rise in fraud] was due to a gradual erosion of ethics, but it seems to have gone into freefall," he says. Technology, he adds, has only added more weight to the plummet. "Fraud is growing, especially in technological areas. There's software piracy, trademark theft—historically, technology made it more difficult to commit fraud, but now it's easier. All you have to do, for example, is buy a $4,000 machine and you can copy encyclopedias for a few cents and flog them for hundreds or thousands of dollars. The twenty-four-hour nature of the markets is also going to enhance opportunities for fraud in all market areas."

Moulton points to the move away from a cash-based society to a cashless society through electronic money transfer as a means for fraudsters to dupe the public and bag serious money. "The ability to duplicate bits and bytes means the opportunities are enormous," he says.

He also believes the intrinsic "sexiness" of securities-market fraud has attracted a lot more white-collar criminals. He believes the public has become almost immune to story after story about "some guy in red suspenders" making off with a pile of cash. "The jargon in the market, like 'uptick and downtick,' it's such an esoteric thing. There's a perception portrayed by the media that makes these guys so flashy. It would be equally possible to denigrate what they do, but it wouldn't sell papers.... Bare bones, it's just lies, lies and more damn lies," he says.

Moulton thinks, however, that authorities could do more to apprehend the bad guys, even though their hands are tied by budget and jurisdictional constraints. "We [the police] are the only aspect of the criminal justice system that deal with all of the players. We deal with the victims, we deal with the accused. We deal with the means by which the offence is committed. We deal with the lawyers. We deal with the jail people. Nobody else does that. We have a perspective to offer the court, but we've never somehow sold that.... It's very easy in terms of a stabbing or a hold-up or a rape to say, 'This is the victim, this is what happened.' We haven't done that in terms of the people who are victims of fraud. There's a faceless mass out there, or you have an equally faceless entity like a bank. To say that a bank is a victim is a pretty hard sell anywhere. But we haven't taken it that one step further. And we haven't sold the inherent aspects of imposing a sentence because so much of this crime can be committed by so many people."

Another RCMP officer, Sgt. John Sliter, dug even deeper into the problem—at least from the RCMP's perspective. Sliter's thesis, "A Policy Review of the Role of the Royal Canadian Mounted Police in Securities Fraud Enforcement," which he completed in 1994 for his master's degree in business, addressed the issues surrounding fraud and the RCMP's history in handling

# Conclusion

the crime with remarkable candour.

"There are a number of reasons for the ineffectiveness of the securities fraud enforcement strategy," he writes. "There are also jurisdictional struggles between different levels of government and within government departments ... and a number of internal RCMP problems, in particular in the area of human resources policy. A survey of RCMP securities fraud investigators determined that for the most part they are not equipped to investigate major securities frauds. They are lacking in formal education, specialized training, and generally do not remain within the section long enough to become proficient and complete a major investigation."

Sliter's work, supported by many interviews he conducted with RCMP officers across the country, shines a bright light on a less-than-perfect system. Comments from RCMP officers illustrate some of their concerns and frustrations:

"The transfer of trained personnel out of market function through promotion [or frustration] seriously hampers continuity and loses expertise," said Const. G. Fraser of Calgary.

"I believe we are too reactive. We wait for complaints as opposed to using sources to determine where the problems are and developing operational plans to attack the problem.... We have to be prepared to take risks and be inventive in our approaches," added Sgt. Brian Tario of Winnipeg. (Tario was one of the investigating officers in the Winnipeg Commodity Exchange–related frauds described in Chapter 3.)

"In six years I have yet to see a major file completed by the members who initiated same," said Sgt. Alec Popovic, Toronto.

Sgt. Sliter believes that to effectively deter securities fraudsters, "there must be genuine risk of being discovered, prosecuted and incarcerated." In Canada, for example, convicted felons of non-violent crimes such as fraud only serve one-third of their sentences before being able to seek day parole, and can be freed on statutory release after serving two-thirds of the time. For sentences of two years or more, federal parole rules permit release even earlier. Sliter says "there is a strong need for national enforcement. Criminal securities-fraud investigations are generally international and are always national in scope." Unlike securities markets in the United States, which are overseen by the Securities and Exchange Commission, or similarly, in Britain by the Serious Fraud Office, Canada minds its securities business on a province-by-province basis—at least for the moment. Federal-provincial talks about forming a national body, which have been simmering for decades, are once again heating up. A federal regulatory commission is a contentious issue for regulators across Canada. Some say a unified securities body is unnecessary and would infringe on the provinces' rights. Critics also say the cost benefits would be negligible, and that a single regulatory commission would allow Canada's major national banks—all six of which run some form of securities operation— to gain too much influence.

Representatives from commissions in Ontario, Quebec, British Columbia and Alberta, the four provinces with the biggest securities exchanges in Canada, have been the most vocal about the issue. A federal regulatory body will mean "one-stop shopping for prospectuses, registrations and redemptions, and that's

# Conclusion

about it. Are they going to be smarter regulators with the Feds? No. Are they going to be better regulators? No," says Dean Holley, former executive director of the British Columbia Securities Commission who is now a consultant. Quebec Securities Commission chairman Jean Martel said in a speech in the spring of 1996 that the federal proposal "seems to hold all the ingredients for a dizzying increase in costs."

Whether the provinces ultimately agree on one national body remains to be seen. But there have been lessons learned in the face of a changing securities landscape in Canada and around the world. Despite tighter funding and turf squabbles, groups across the country and between Canada and the U.S. are taking the initiative to find ways to do a more effective job. One example is a pilot project that started in September 1995 in British Columbia. Its mandate is to "develop a meaningful criminal deterrent," says Mark Skwarok, former chief legal counsel of the province's Securities Commission. Skwarok says the goal is to pull together a fifteen-person team of five prosecutors and ten RCMP investigators who are "dedicated to fighting securities crime.... We want to increase awareness, both in the courts and in the investment industry, so that we can get convictions. That's the only way we'll send a message."

Another initiative launched by Industry Canada and the U.S. Federal Trade Commission (FTC) in the fall of 1996 formed a task force to crack down on cross-border false marketing practices. The goal is to stop fraudsters from setting up shop in one country and targeting citizens in another.

Still another group is the Securities Enforcement Review Committee (SERC), which was formed in June 1996 and is made up of representatives from the RCMP, the Ontario Provincial

Police, the Metropolitan Toronto Police Fraud Squad, the Toronto Stock Exchange (TSE), the Ontario Securities Commission (OSC), the Investment Dealers Association of Canada (IDA) and the Ontario Ministry of the Attorney General, to deal more efficiently with securities-related cases. Fredric Maefs, director of the enforcement division of the TSE and a committee member of SERC, says it should help cut down on costs and enable investigators to discern which cases have the best chance of being prosecuted. "At the TSE we have zero tolerance for member firms who fail to correct deficiences in compliance, financial or market matters, but we also recognize that we have to work with the Ministry of the Attorney General, the police and SROs [self-regulating organizations like the OSC and the IDA] to do a better job." Maefs said the TSE, for one, plans to "seek higher penalties" for all securities-related crimes.

Detective Staff Inspector Stephen Harris, who until recently headed the Metropolitan Toronto Police Fraud Squad and served as the force's representative on SERC, admits that even though fighting fraud is an uphill climb, the lack of funding, ironically, "has forced us to become more innovative. We've had to find ways to work with other law-enforcement and regulatory groups, which hasn't entirely been a bad thing." However, he is quick to add that the squad would never say no to more money if it came their way.

Money—or lack of it—is a big issue for regulators and police, but even those who defend the people charged with fraud would like to see more government funds spent in the process. David Humphrey, a partner at Greenspan, Humphrey in Toronto, says that "from a very selfish perspective I'd like to see the RCMP and the Ministry of the Attorney General fully funded so that

# Conclusion

every case of alleged fraud is vigorously prosecuted. I'll end up with a lot more clients in my office." Humphrey may get his wish—at least part of it. According to OSC representatives, the Ontario government is planning to establish self-funding at the Commission by the fall of 1997. This would provide more money to hire additional staff to investigate alleged fraud cases. Humphrey, who defended fallen investment broker Christopher Horne (Chapter 5), and whose law firm is acting on behalf of Allen Grossman, charged in the gemstone case involving victims from the Pennsylvania area (Chapter 1), notes that the potentially huge costs to prosecute many of these cases is a major consideration for the prosecution. "I see the cases that are being prosecuted, particularly by the Crown law office, and I see them being very effectively prosecuted. Certainly, there are some financial limits in how they conduct the prosecution. A forensic accounting is usually done through the victims or the employer of the accused. Optimally, the Crown would like to prosecute the case and have available to it an independent forensic accountant, not one connected with the victims or the accused's employer. The reality is that independent forensic accountings can cost hundreds of thousands of dollars. The Crown just can't afford to spend those amounts on every case."

As governments, regulators and the legal system grapple with fraud from the outside, there are still others who are doing their part within companies. Glenn Higginbotham, vice-president, Corporate Compliance, Corporate and Legal Affairs, at the Bank of Montreal, admits it may be an old-fashioned notion, but if senior management set a good example, staff aren't as likely to turn to fraud as a means to supplement their income.

"It's very key to an organization to not only have a strong

# GREED

leader, but an ethical leader, if you're going to operate a bank where public trust is so important," Higginbotham says. He credits Matthew Barrett, the bank's chairman and chief executive officer, and Tony Comper, president and chief operating officer, for showing exactly this sort of leadership.

Higginbotham believes that internal control systems and moral leadership must also go hand in hand in order to instil—as much as possible—ethical behaviour in all employees. "Tony Comper and Matthew Barrett set the example ... but we also have systems in place, like when we started off monitoring securities trading [the bank completed its purchase of brokerage firm Nesbitt Burns in 1992]. We set out limits on what people could do, and on what business activities employees could get involved in."

The bank, like a growing number of companies including all of the major banks in Canada, asks employees to annually review the firm's code of conduct, which Higginbotham describes as "the lowest common denominator of awareness you need." Among other initiatives, the Bank of Montreal conducts regular employee opinion surveys that ask staff if they feel they've received appropriate guidance in terms of behaviour, for themselves and others on staff.

But this is an area, says Higginbotham, where the waters become muddied for most companies, including banks, and that's how to deal with whistleblowers. "I don't think you'll find any whistleblowing program among any of the banks that is really significant," he says. "We have an anonymous way to ask questions (and point out perceived problems and problem-makers). But we're still working on that program. What really surprises me are the number of people here who do come forward. It all goes back to the culture of the organization. The culture must offer enough security for someone to point out wrongdoers. If you have a culture where everyone knows what the rules are and what is expected of them, then people will point out things that they think are amiss. Corporate culture really flows from the top, right back to the CEO," Higginbotham says.

Few would find fault in that point. But the blunt reality is that, generally, whistleblowers aren't a well-loved breed in the corporate world. According to recent statistics from the Association of Medical Health Specialists in College Park, Maryland, 82 per cent of whistleblowers suffer some form of corporate harassment. As many as 60 per cent are fired, 17 per cent lose their houses because of job loss since it is especially difficult for them to secure another position without references. Astonishingly, 10 per cent of the whistleblowers surveyed reported that they not only contemplated but actually attempted suicide.

It's perverse that many "legitimate" whistleblowers—people who can prove that they know of someone in the company or markets who is doing something illegal—find themselves worse off than those who committed the corporate thefts or frauds. David Threlkeld, the thirty-year metals-trading veteran who blew the whistle on copper trader Yasuo Hamanaka of Sumitomo— one of his company's most important clients—said "because nothing was done [at first] against Sumitomo, I was hung out to dry." Threlkeld said he was ostracized by other copper-market traders throughout the entire ordeal. There are others, however, like Mark Whitacre, a one-time senior executive at Archer-Daniels Midland Co., the U.S. grain processor that was found guilty of price-fixing in October 1996 and fined US $100 million. He blew the whistle on the firm and became an FBI informant in the case but he, along with two other company executives, was also indicted by a federal grand jury in December 1996 for conspiring to fix prices of the feed additive lysine.

Part of the concern over whistleblowing is that companies are hesitant about declaring open season on anyone who *appears* to be doing something out of the ordinary, or providing a forum for those on staff with an axe to grind against other co-workers. As the Bank of Montreal's Higginbotham says, "striking the right balance" between establishing enough controls and encouraging open dialogue is the primary goal but one that can prove difficult to achieve.

Higginbotham says the need to implement appropriate controls has become even more acute since legislation in the '80s gave banks the green light to provide a wider spectrum of financial services, including securities and investment advice. He points out that banks have historically conveyed a conservative message, even to the point of being blatantly paternalistic. "Strict controls were put in place because of perceived abuses that might arise. Even what were thought to be 'inappropriate' marriages [among staff] were regarded as a threat of some sort.... But one of the key things for a bank to convey is public trust, and even though some of the earlier rules were rather archaic, management knew that once trust was lost ... you'd soon find yourself out of business."

(Obviously, the times they aren't a-changin' all that quickly. The bank learned the hard way when it launched a controversial promotional ad in the fall of '96 that featured children singing '60s icon Bob Dylan's tune "The Times They Are A-Changin'." Many disgruntled customers felt that the song, which is about changing the social order, was inappropriately used to push a new electronic banking service, mbanx—and they made their feelings known to staff.)

This is a good example of how "previously polite" investors are now raising their voices and demanding more—and not just bigger dividends or changes in advertising—from the companies in which they own shares. They are also seeking answers from senior executives about corporate codes of ethics and accountability. When employees, for example, commit fraud and steal money from clients, or significantly misuse the power of their position for their own benefit, they ask—who is culpable? Is it just the employees, or does it include management and, perhaps, even the board of directors?

There are no easy answers and much depends on the circumstances surrounding the fraudulent or illegal acts. For example, the British arm of Coopers & Lybrand, auditors for the ill-fated Barings Bank, filed a third-party lawsuit against nine former directors of the bank in late 1996, saying it wasn't just former trader Nick Leeson who was to blame, but also senior management who weren't keeping a proper eye on him. "Despite the fact that we are not responsible for the collapse of Barings, we face a substantial claim. We are perceived to have deep pockets which are available to those who have lost money while those who were really responsible for the collapse of Barings escape," said a Coopers statement. Another example is money manager Veronika Hirsch, who became a "star" through a media campaign, and was wooed away from Toronto-based mutual fund company AGF to Fidelity Investments, the world's largest mutual fund firm. While at AGF, she appears to have bent industry and company rules to make personal trades in Oliver Gold, a Vancouver-based junior mining company, which netted her a profit of around $250,000. She was clearly skating on the edge. (Both the British Columbia and the Ontario Securities Commissions are looking into the matter.) A review of investment manager practices by the Investment Funds Institute of Canada, an industry watchdog following the Hirsch incident, in part suggested that there is a need for "ethics police" in both the industry in general and, ideally, at every investment fund company.

David Selley, a partner at Ernst & Young and president of the Canadian Centre for Ethics & Corporate Policy, agrees and adds that "if there isn't anybody checking up, you're almost giving employees more temptation."

Another challenge in the money management industry is that a good number of its more talented professionals—and many of those who are not that gifted—are driven by ego, which is an obligatory characteristic of those who must daily take risks in the markets. The difficulty is that some end up believing their own press and step over the boundaries of what is acceptable behaviour. In the past, management at investment firms tended to offer their mavericks unbridled open spaces. But that's changing. Creating "teams" of investment professionals who work together in a collegial relationship is now occurring with far more regularity.

The responsibility of boards of directors is also being held up to closer scrutiny. No longer the domain of corpulent old boys prone to eating, snoozing and rubber-stamping their way through quarterly and annual meetings, most of today's directors are expected to sit up and take notice of what's going on at the company. "Bored" directors are no longer tolerated.

Sir Graham Day, an authority on corporate governance who currently serves as an independent director on several public and private companies, is a prime example of the "new" breed of directors. He sits on the boards of Jebsens S.A., the Laird Group plc and the EMI Group plc, the Bank of Nova Scotia, CSL Group Inc., Extendicare Inc., Empire Co. Ltd., Nova Corp. and the Shaw Group Ltd. Sir Graham, who is a dual-national, Canadian–British, and was knighted in 1989 by Queen Elizabeth for his services to British industry, also brings to his extensive board responsibilities an impressive corporate pedigree. Currently chancellor of Dalhousie University in Nova Scotia, he retired in 1993 as chairman of Cadbury Schweppes plc and of PowerGen plc, and was, successively, chairman and chief executive of British Shipbuilders and of the Rover Group plc. From September 1991 until May 1992 he was chairman of British Aerospace plc on an interim basis during a period of management and strategic realignment.

Sir Graham has some very strong views on the responsibilities of directors, especially when discussing corporate fraud prevention. "It starts right down at the minutiae. Where regulators have suggested that directors are the ultimate safeguard against fraud, well they're just whistling Dixie. Directors can and should make sure the systems are in place that both minimize the opportunities and maximize the chances of detection. But the possibility that directors, whether individually or collectively, might all of a sudden say, 'Eureka! Branch manager X has his arm in the till up to the armpit,' isn't very likely. Directors manage the managers. Even as a senior manager, you're not going to detect everything that's not right," Sir Graham says.

Nonetheless, Sir Graham strongly believes that "senior management has the highest responsibility because they, by and large, are the people who are visible to all of the employees, or if they're not visible, they should be." He says it is counter-productive for a board of directors to micromanage a company, but that the board is very much obligated to "ensure that procedures and controls are in place" and are functioning properly within the corporation.

"Corporate governance, of course, is being distorted to cover a much wider waterfront by regulators and legislators, most of whom have never served on the board of a very large listed company. It's like the virgin writing the handbook for behaviour in the brothel, you can be strong on theory, but the practice is quite different," he says candidly. "It's the same with university professors. I can't think of many names of professors at universities who are now running courses on corporate governance who've ever sat on any boards of any size. They can say, 'this is right, or this is wrong,' but in the jungle it's very different."

A lot of people agree with Sir Graham, but the subject also tends to provoke disparate views. In its final report released in December 1994, the TSE Committee on Corporate Governance in Canada raised some senior executives' blood pressures along Bay Street when it recommended that a company's board should be made up of "a majority of unrelated directors." The report, spearheaded by former OSC chairman Peter Dey, went on to say that "the inclusion of management on board committees should be the exception rather than the rule reflecting our belief ... of the importance of the board being able to function independently of management."

Like several other company executives from a wide cross-section of Canadian firms, Ronald Greene, chairman of Renaissance Energy Ltd., argued otherwise: "A management director is an important source of input and perspective to every

# Conclusion

committee. To ensure every committee's independence it should be at least balanced or overweighted by outside directors.... A management director's input should be viewed as an asset, not a liability. If it is the latter, then the board must question whether it is effectively constituted," he said.

The TSE's Ralph Shay, V.P. of company listings and regulation, defends the report, saying that "we always have to emphasize that the exchange is not requiring companies to follow any of these guidelines. There's a recognition that they're not suitable for every company, particularly smaller companies.... But the very process of going through the guidelines, even if companies don't adhere to all of them, has made an improvement. A couple of years ago very few companies had corporate governance committees. Now, a lot of firms are saying that they're introducing more independent outside directors ... there's also a genuine desire to improve corporate governance."

He adds that "part of the public's concern is that boards of companies that are controlled by a large single shareholder tend to be influenced by that shareholder." That's true, but fortunately today the likes of a Robert Maxwell, the now-deceased British publishing magnate who was accused of stealing $1 billion from employee pension funds to prop up weak corporate holdings, are the exception to the rule. Nevertheless, Sir Graham believes it is imperative to ensure that everyone in the corporation, regardless of rank, must adhere to responsible and ethical behaviour.

He describes a situation that happened at Rover when he was the luxury car-maker's chairman and chief executive: "Most of the time if you're a manager, you have a much better chance to detect a fraud than you do if you're a director. In this one incident there was a chap running Rover's motor sport division.

Now, the very nature of motor sport means that you're doing a lot of things on a cash basis. But this chap just seemed to have a lifestyle that was not supported by the kind of money he was earning. However, I'd set up a good internal audit system and we caught him." Investigators eventually discovered that the employee had swindled half a million pounds from the company and owned lavish homes in Spain and England.

Sir Graham also raises the point that senior personnel must not be part of or tolerate a double standard. "A lot of companies choose to try and bury a problem because they believe their own corporate image will be harmed if the world sees someone on staff has taken them for a lot of money. It doesn't matter where the person who committed the crime is in the hierarchy. Bang— if someone steps out of line, and if you've got the evidence, you prosecute because that's the proper thing to do."

Sir Graham's beyond-reproach reputation is in part due to the lessons he learned while at Cadbury Schweppes plc. A protégé of Sir Adrian Cadbury, also a former chairman of the company as well as a world-renowned expert on corporate governance, Sir Graham literally learned at the side of a master. The Cadbury family, heirs to a fortune built on chocolate, have roots back to the Quaker movement, which helped form Sir Adrian's high principles. Sir Graham says that his mentor showed him that appropriate behaviour "is not rocket science. It really comes down to individual morality. Sir Adrian now tells me that he's forgotten he said this, but it was just so compelling. Someone, a young employee, had asked him whether he would know the right thing to do if he were faced with a situation. Sir Adrian looked at this person and said, 'If you have to ask the question, the answer is—No.'"

# Appendix: To Catch a Thief

According to ethics and fraud experts, when it comes to morality we each fall into a particular category. Only about 20 per cent of us never slip from the moral high ground and *always* tell the truth. At the opposite end of the spectrum, there's another 20 per cent who always "look for ways to beat the system," says Gary Moulton of Deloitte & Touche. "The rest of us fall somewhere in between the two extremes."

Not surprisingly, people who commit fraud tend to fall into the "beat-the-system" category. There are certain red flags to watch for, however, to make detecting those committing fraud a little easier:

- A fraudster tends to have "a big ego and isn't afraid to flaunt it. These people crave the best and like to lord it over others, or at least exaggerate their self-importance," says Moulton.

- They may have a substance-abuse problem or gambling addiction.

- They live way beyond their means and often buy big-ticket items.

- They're self-absorbed and superficial in their dealings with others.

- They tend to be unusually hard-working and reluctant to take vacations for fear of their scam being discovered.

- They may have severe marital problems and heavy debt loads which put them under huge financial pressures.

- They may be subject to sudden mood swings or personality changes.

It is important to remember that the vast majority of investment professionals are acting in your best interests. However, even though regulatory and police agencies are battling the crime, consumers must learn to protect and educate themselves. Here are some useful tips:

- Don't buy anything over the phone *unless you've initiated the call*. Don't give out personal information, such as credit card numbers, bank account information, annual income, etc., to any caller who wishes to sell you something out of the blue.

- Don't fall for anyone claiming that you've won something but that you must first pay "taxes" or "fees" in order to receive your gift. If it's a proper contest, you shouldn't need to send money to obtain the prize.

- If you're not sure that the individual calling you is a legitimate salesperson, take their name, telephone number and company name and don't buy anything until they've been thoroughly checked out. If they're selling stocks, gems or any other "investment" you're not familiar with, just say "no thank you" and hang up. If they call again, warn them that you'll call the authorities and take action if they bother you further.

# Appendix: To Catch a Thief

- Senior citizens and people with limited access to the outside world must be especially careful. As tempting as an investment offer might seem, if it sounds too good to be true, it usually is. All of the Big Six Canadian banks have some form of investment counselling arm, and your bank manager should be able to put you in touch with a qualified investment professional. However, independent investment firms both small and large, such as Midland Walwyn, have solid reputations, too. Be sure to check them out. Regardless of which way you go, ask friends and family for referrals and find out if they're happy with their broker or portfolio manager. If you want to invest and don't have a whole lot of money, mutual funds are a good option, but be sure to choose funds with a strong track record that are suited to your investment needs and risk tolerance. *The Globe and Mail* and *The Financial Post*, both national newspapers, regularly offer special reports on mutual funds, and there are several good books on the subject. Contact your local library or bookstore for more information.

- Check monthly and quarterly account statements. If you're not sure what everything means, ask your banker, broker or money manager to explain. Don't be afraid to ask—it's your money and you need to know what's happening to it. If you catch anything that you think isn't correct, call the investment professional you're dealing with and tell them. If you don't get a satisfactory answer, contact management at the firm and complain. Don't allow yourself to be pushed aside.

- Surfing the Internet? Don't give out any personal information unless you've checked the Website with appropriate authorities. Remember, cyberspace is borderless—if you're a victim of fraud via the Internet there's usually very little you can do to retrieve your losses or fight back.

Contact your local regulatory agency if you need more information about securities-related matters, investment firms or if you wish to file a complaint. The telephone numbers of securities commissions across Canada are:

**Alberta**
Edmonton, Alberta
Tel. (403) 427-5201

Calgary, Alberta
Tel. (403) 297-6454

**British Columbia**
Vancouver, British Columbia
Tel. (604) 660-4800

**Manitoba**
Winnipeg, Manitoba
Tel. (204) 945-2548

**New Brunswick**
Saint John, New Brunswick
Tel. (506) 658-3060

**Newfoundland**
St. John's, Newfoundland
Tel. (709) 729-4189

**Northwest Territories**
Yellowknife, Northwest
Territories
Tel. (403) 920-3318

**Nova Scotia**
Halifax, Nova Scotia
Tel. (902) 424-7768

**Ontario**
Toronto, Ontario
Tel. (416) 597-0681

**Prince Edward Island**
Charlottetown,
Prince Edward
Island
Tel: (902) 368-4550

**Quebec**
Montreal, Quebec
Tel. (514) 873-5326

# Appendix: To Catch a Thief

**Saskatchewan**
Regina, Saskatchewan
Tel. (306) 787-5645

**Yukon**
Whitehorse, Yukon
(403) 667-5005

Other resources include the Canadian Securities Institute, which is an educational organization sponsored by the Investment Dealers Association of Canada, and the Montreal, Toronto, Alberta and Vancouver Stock Exchanges. You can contact the CSI for more information on investing at these numbers:

Toronto (416) 364-9130; Montreal (514) 878-3591;
Calgary (403) 262-1791; Vancouver (604) 683-1338.

If you have questions about U.S.-based brokers or investment firms, you may call the (U.S.) National Association of Securities Dealers. For general inquiries call (301) 590-6500. Their hotline number is 1-800-289-9999.

The U.S. Securities and Exchange Commission's general number is (202) 942-8090; their consumer protection number is (202) 942-7040.

# INDEX

# Index

# Index

# Index